"In our world, having bundles of cas[h]
[ac]quiring assets remains a constant temptation for the church and its ministers. In this book, Conley Owens offers a timely challenge for how those who claim to be servants of Christ should handle money in carrying out their ministry. This work is biblically grounded, stimulating, and bold. Highly recommended!"

 —**David E. Garland**, professor of Christian Scriptures, George W. Truett Theological Seminary

"If more churches and Christian organizations would follow the principles outlined in this book, many of the financial scandals that have plagued Christianity in recent years could have been avoided. Further, we would develop a deeper trust in God's provision, celebrate how God has supplied, and spend more time actually doing the work of ministry instead of raising funds for ministry."

 —**S. Michael Houdmann**, founder and president of Got Questions Ministries

"Conley Owens wonders if Christian fund-raising is, or even can be, Christian. As he shows by careful attention to biblical teaching on money and its use, this question could not be more pertinent for the many Christian enterprises that today engage so creatively in such activity. It is certainly an imperative for believers to support Christian institutions with their money, but, as this well-argued book suggests, maybe not in the ways that are now commonplace."

 —**Mark A. Noll**, co-editor of *More Money, More Ministry: Money and Evangelicals in Recent North American History*

"The author challenges the status quo and dares to ask very hard (and awkward) questions. He does a careful job of dealing with the biblical texts and their application to how ministry is funded. His diagrams and personal illustrations are helpful. While I agree with many of the concerns he raises, I also appreciate his charitable attitude towards those (including myself) who may not fully embrace each of his conclusions."

 —**Jim Newheiser**, author of *Money, Debt, and Finances: Critical Questions and Answers*

"This book will raise questions—the right ones. I'm still thinking through the concepts and implications that author Conley Owens has pushed from his side of the table to ours for examination. For years, I have been looking at how cultural perceptions about money collide with Scripture. This book will demand your attention similarly. I will recommend it often."

 —**Jim Elliff**, president of Christian Communicators Worldwide

"How you handle money in ministry can be evidence of being a faithful servant of the Lord or a false teacher. Conley Owens takes up the challenge of how to properly support the Lord's work financially in this engaging book. Instead of just offering his best opinions, Owens interacts with the Bible's teaching on the subject, down to the details. After seeking to master the Scriptural data, he works out his conclusions practically, answering real-life scenarios. Even if you don't agree with all of the author's conclusions, you will value the opportunity to interact with his clear-headed, Bible-based arguments."

—**John Crotts**, pastor of Faith Bible Church of Sharpsburg, GA

"'Freely you have received, freely give,' Jesus told his disciples as they prepared for gospel work. How Christian ministers and ministries are funded, however, can either undermine or underscore Jesus' exhortation. In *The Dorean Principle*, Conley Owens shows us that Scripture consistently forbids reciprocity when it comes to ministry fundraising. Spiritual instruction should always be given without pay, and those who make their living by the gospel should be supplied by those who are *joining* them in their work, not paying them for it. This is an important book that I pray will help many Christian ministries change their fundraising practices for the better."

—**Derek Brown**, academic dean of The Cornerstone Bible College and Seminary

"*The Dorean Principle* presents the high standard for ministry fundraising that can be seen throughout scripture and especially in the teaching and lives of Jesus and Paul. Despite spending my entire career as a Christian working on free and open source software, I found its applications to software/content licensing to be particularly thought-provoking and unexpectedly challenging. Conley Owens is thorough in his research, sound in his analysis, and unapologetic in his challenge for how we should apply this principle in our own pursuits of gospel ministry."

—**Will Norris**, open source lead at Twitter

"As an open source software developer of almost two decades, while reading *The Dorean Principle*, I found myself saying, "yes... yes... YES!" Conley Owens's book eloquently expresses my motivation to freely develop software for the church. More than that, *The Dorean Principle* highlights problems and offers potential solutions for Christians, churches, authors, and seminaries when dealing with money."

—**Raoul Snyman**, creator and maintainer of OpenLP worship presentation software

"Conley Owens has written an accessible, conversation-starting work that has the potential to turn the operations of the modern church upside down. It is easy to call out the excess we see in the financial enterprises that exist within the church in America, but until now there has not been a simplified analysis of the foundational principles at play. How different is our favorite author's business model from that of the "health and wealth" charlatans that plague daytime television? *The Dorean Principle* is a necessary look in the mirror for the entire American Evangelical project. We need to work out the details and Conley provides some bare-knuckled input on that front. Things cannot continue the same for long after we digest this biblical study on fundraising in ministry. I highly recommend this book and believe it is a much-needed paradigm shift in how we think about money and ministry."
 —**AD Robles**, host of the AD Robles podcast

"In the many years I have spent helping ministers establish a presence on the Internet, misguided concerns about money have been the biggest hindrance. This book uniquely and powerfully addresses those concerns, capturing the biblical principles that have guided my labors. On account of these same principles, John Piper gave me permission to freely share his sermons through the website that blossomed into the online ministry of Desiring God. He chose faith over bean counting, and God has provided."
 —**Moe Bergeron**, Internet evangelism pioneer

"More than ever before, Christian fundraising in the modern church has become a worldly, unethical, scandalous scheme. These kinds of unbiblical practices are typically connected with unbiblical false teachers and leaders. Scripture devotes much space to the problem and temptation of *philarguros* ('lovers of silver,' 2 Tim. 3:2). Conley Owens has done a fantastic service for the church in *The Dorean Principle*. Owens outlines in detail, faith-centric, biblically prescribed fundraising, contra unprincipled and manipulative fundraising, of which he provides many examples. I highly recommend *The Dorean Principle* especially to church leaders and Christian organizations."
 —**Edward Dalcour**, president of the Department of Christian Defense

"*The Dorean Principle* offers a carefully nuanced interpretation of Scripture's teaching on the relationship between money and gospel ministry, suggesting a helpful resolution to the tension between a laborer being worthy of his wages and his obligation to minister free of charge. The work deserves careful consideration and re-reading."
 —**Brandon Adams**, blogger at contrast2.wordpress.com

"Conley Owens boldly addresses what the Bible says about funding Christian ministry. Carefully consider what he writes. I have found that God is faithful to His Word, and the principles He set forth in the Holy Bible can fully be relied on."

—**Michael Paul Johnson**, senior editor of the *World English Bible*

"Owens addresses the important topic of funding Christian ministry with candor and helpful insights from Scripture. Content creators and translators who are interested in the advance of God's Kingdom to the ends of the earth will benefit from careful consideration of his application of biblical principles to the issue of copyright licensing."

—**Tim Jore**, author of *The Christian Commons: Ending the Spiritual Famine of the Global Church*

"Looking to Matthew 10:8–10 and similar passages, Conley Owens carefully delineates between the notions of "reciprocity" and "colabor." Rather than merely defining and defending this principle, he also engages in applying it in real, present day situations, proposing solutions. This book is not designed to be the final answer and perfect fix, but to provoke further exploration of the subject in God's Word and to urge probing dialogue and discerning decision making. Indeed, I commend this book for this purpose."

—**Jason Deutsch**, chancellor of Providence Evangelical Bible Seminary, India

"Should we *charge* for ministry? Sounds preposterous, doesn't it? Yet, this is exactly what takes place on a daily basis in multiple contexts throughout Christendom, from conferences to counseling. In this timely and much-needed work, Pastor Owens challenges us to consider the true nature of Christian ministry and reform our ministry finances accordingly. The Christian ministry must be viewed as it is presented to us in the New Testament—the gospel has been *entrusted* to us. Pastors are not peddlers, but ambassadors and stewards. Freely we have received; let us therefore freely give!"

—**John H. McDonald**, president of The Log College & Seminary

The Dorean Principle

The Dorean Principle

*A Biblical Response
to the
Commercialization of Christianity*

Conley Owens

The Dorean Principle: A Biblical Response to the Commercialization of Christianity

2021, Conley Owens

Published by FirstLove Publications
P.O. Box 2190
Dublin, CA 94568

Cover design: Matthew Sample II
Editing: Carissa Early

Unless otherwise indicated, all Scripture quotations are from the ESV® Bible (The Holy Bible, English Standard Version®), copyright © 2001 by Crossway, a publishing ministry of Good News Publishers. Used by permission. All rights reserved.

Scripture quotations marked "NASB" taken from the New American Standard Bible® (NASB), Copyright © 1960, 1962, 1963, 1968, 1971, 1972, 1973, 1975, 1977, 1995 by The Lockman Foundation Used by permission. www.Lockman.org

ISBN: 978-1-953151-15-5 (pbk.)
LCCN: 2021915088

21 22 23 24 25 26 27 28 29 30 31   10 9 8 7 6 5 4 3 2

For Lee and Lila Owens,
whose spirit of charity shaped me as well as this book

Contents

List of Figures

Foreword

To my knowledge, a book like this has never been written. Bits and pieces of its truth have been scattered throughout the large body of Christian literature over the centuries, but none has ever written a book devoted entirely to showing the relationship between money and ministry. One wonders why this book wasn't written centuries ago since two thousand years of church history shows a shameful record of reproach brought on by greedy teachers, those who use their knowledge of God's word to personally profit and cause gainsayers' occasion to blaspheme the name of the Lord.

Since 2006, FirstLove Publications has given away over 300,000 copies of publications to souls hungry for the word of God. This, of course, is our reasonable service. We deserve no special accolades for obeying the commands to "preach the word" (2 Tim. 4:2) and "freely give" (Matt. 10:8). However, by the free distribution of the word of God, we are assured we cannot be rightly accused of making merchandise of God's word. On the contrary, we can cite examples of God's word bringing forth much fruit for His glory. This brings comfort to the conscience.

Our methods matter. In other words, the tactics we employ to increase the kingdom of God must arise from sound theology. In such a holy enterprise, the ends do not justify the means. When our works are tested on judgment day, many will be surprised to find much of their works rooted in selfish, greedy motives.

> Let each one take care how he builds upon it. For no
> one can lay a foundation other than that which is laid,
> which is Jesus Christ. Now if anyone builds on the

foundation with gold, silver, precious stones, wood, hay, straw—each one's work will become manifest, for the Day will disclose it, because it will be revealed by fire, and the fire will test what sort of work each one has done. (1 Cor. 3:10b–13).

The challenge this book provides will not discourage you in God's vineyard but inspire you further to "test everything; hold fast what is good. Abstain from every form of evil" (1 Thess. 5:21–22). This testing process will result in more lasting fruit and a ministry more useful in the Master's service.

You will find *The Dorean Principle* to be undergirded with theological and biblical accuracy. Carefully researched with attention to detail and depth of insight, the value of this book cannot be overstated.

Joseph M. Jacowitz
President, FirstLove Ministries

Introduction

A Call for Discernment

Consider the sheer quantity of wealth that changes hands in the name of Christ. Christian book sales climb into the hundreds of millions of dollars.[1] Parachurch ministries amass sizable revenues, with organizations like Cru surpassing $600 million.[2] Seminaries often collect tuition upwards of $60,000 for a standard degree, with loan payments leaving many pastors financially shackled for years. Even small-dollar transactions impose their own heavy burdens. For example, church leaders exhaust countless hours wrestling to understand and purchase the appropriate licenses to worship music in order to accommodate the needs of their congregation. Certainly, money fuels the work of ministry, and the worker is worthy of his wages (1 Tim. 5:18), but at what point does the financial enterprise go too far?

The modern church lacks the moral parameters necessary to identify ethical transgressions in ministry fundraising. Of course, who wouldn't object to the money-grubbing solicitations of prosperity gospel preachers and aberrant televangelists? But our judgment must extend beyond the ability to detect the most egregious infractions. In a context where biblical discernment is limited, ministry leaders operate without guidance or real accountability. Now, more than ever, the church must turn to the word of God to find wisdom on these matters and develop the clarity required for true discernment.

---

[1]Nielsen, *Focusing on our Strengths.*
[2]Cru, *2018 Annual Report.*

The goal of this brief book is to establish "the dorean principle," a biblical precept that distinguishes ethical ministry fundraising from unethical ministry fundraising. The dorean principle characterizes godly financial activity in the name of the gospel as acts of colabor in contradistinction to acts of reciprocity. Ministry should be supported, not sold.

Our primary instruction comes from the words of Jesus, Paul, and other apostles as they teach the dorean principle. The early church corroborates our findings by practicing in accord with its dictates. Finally, we will make some practical applications and chart a path forward to resist the commercialization of Christianity. In the end, I hope this study will be as enlightening for you as it was for me, and that you will find yourself closer to answering the enigma that intersects ministry and money.

I write these words in order to address a topic that for too long has not received the attention it deserves—a topic often outright avoided. This book is not the final word on the matter but rather a first attempt at capturing a biblical ethic of ministry fundraising. If the Lord chooses to bless this work, it will only be a launching pad for further biblical exploration, application, and discussion. May God guide your thoughts as you read.

> One gives freely, yet grows all the richer;
>   another withholds what he should give, and only suf-
> fers want. (Prov. 11:24)

The Command of Christ

Reciprocity vs. Colabor

When I was 6-years-old, I had a King James Version Bible with the words of Christ marked in red. So many pages consisted only of dull black, so when I would arrive at those pages with crimson verses, I felt that I had stumbled upon a great treasure. Years later, I learned that the gospels were not originally printed in books with color or other typographic novelties but simply penned in whatever ink was available. Moreover, as I matured, I recognized that if the apostles and prophets were authoritative messengers sent by God, then the black letters carry all the same weight as the red.

That is not to say that I hadn't stumbled upon a great treasure! Just as certain miracles were reserved for Christ to perform (John 9:32), certain messages were reserved for him to proclaim. Where best to begin but with the words of the Master?

Luke and Matthew

When you consider the financial maintenance of ministers, what passage first comes to mind? If you have studied the Bible for any significant amount of time, it's likely you landed on the phrase in the middle of Luke 10:7, "*the laborer is worthy of his wages.*" Why this particular phrase?

1. It is undeniably catchy. In fact, this adage was already a traditional proverb by the time that Christ first uttered it.[1]
2. It formed the basis for Paul's understanding of the same topic (1 Tim. 5:18). The apostle's ethic is little more than an extensive application of Christ's command.
3. It represents the first clear teaching on the matter, offered at the dawn of Christian ministry.

However, if you take a look at the passage, you will discover that Luke places this instruction alongside the sending out of the seventy disciples,[2] some time after the sending out of the twelve disciples. Although a useful starting point, it would be better to travel back a little further in time and see what Jesus said to the original twelve. In God's providence, Matthew records this for us, albeit in a phrase that garners less popular recognition: "*the laborer deserves his food.*"

> Heal the sick, raise the dead, cleanse lepers, cast out demons. You received without paying; give without pay. Acquire no gold or silver or copper for your belts, no bag for your journey, or two tunics or sandals or a staff, for the laborer deserves his food. (Matt. 10:8–10)

"Food" in Matthew 10:10 coincides with "wages" in Luke 10:7. It makes little practical difference if a traveling disciple receives a denarius or a denarius's worth of bread; both count as compensation for the work done. From this extended imperative in Matthew 10, we can develop an understanding of Christ's teaching on the relationship between money and ministry.

The Question of Payment

Take another look at the passage. Notice anything interesting? It says the disciples are to "give without pay." At first glance, this appears to

---

[1] Harvey, "The Workman is Worthy of His Hire," passim.
[2] Some modern translations record this as seventy-*two* disciples.

conflict with the idea that "the laborer deserves his food." Should the laborer receive wages or not?

It is unthinkable that any coherent speaker—let alone Jesus, the treasure store of wisdom himself—would offer two contradictory approaches in the same breath. We must find some way to resolve these polar injunctions to refuse and to receive.

Before exploring a more fitting resolution, let us first walk through a few less satisfactory options.

Option 1: *Jesus forbids the disciples from taking a miserly approach to their work but permits receiving payment.* The phrase "freely give" may seem to indicate encouragement toward offering ministry bountifully rather than a prohibition against compensation. However, translations that say "give without pay" are not mistaken. The Greek word used here, *dorean*, indicates the giving of something apart from any remuneration. In a context explicitly concerning money, this is the same word Paul uses to describe his gratuitous (freely offered) preaching (2 Cor. 11:7).

Option 2: *Jesus forbids the disciples from receiving pay but permits them to regard themselves as worthy of it.* This option attempts to maintain the honor of ministry while denying its honorariums. On the contrary, in Luke 10:7, Jesus says that because laborers deserve wages, they should *receive* from the one they stay with. Furthermore, the apostle Paul understands this verse to command the support of ministers (1 Tim. 5:17).

Option 3: *Jesus forbids the disciples from requiring pay but permits them to receive pay.* That is, the disciples are fit for remuneration only when they are willing to minister without it. While this may be an attractive solution, it stands at odds with the actual words of the verse. If the disciples may receive payment, why does Jesus tell them to give without pay?

Option 4: *Jesus forbids the disciples from requesting pay but permits them to receive pay.* This proposed solution suffers from the same problems as the preceding option. Moreover, if the disciples may not request payment, why does Jesus tell them to seek out people who will receive and support them (Matt. 10:11–14; Luke 10:5–8)?

Option 5: *Jesus forbids the disciples from accepting money but* *permits them to receive food and lodging.* First, this proposal creates an arbitrary distinction in capital, as though no interchange exists between gold and groceries. Someone who receives one could easily exchange it for the other. Additionally, the solution fails to address the explicit reference to money in Matthew 10:9. The disciples are to rely on others for their financial needs. In fact, by all accounts, the apostle Paul regards this passage as promoting monetary support (1 Tim. 5:17–18).

Option 6: *Jesus forbids the disciples from receiving payment in exchange for miracles but permits them to receive payment in exchange for preaching.* This option wrongly suggests that the disciples might work wonders apart from any proclamation of the gospel. The disciples are to give freely because they have received freely. They have not received miraculous healings but the good news of the kingdom of God.

Option 7: *Jesus forbids the disciples from receiving excess profit but permits them to receive that which meets their needs.* Such a mediating approach fails to satisfy either pole of inquiry. Regarding the command not to receive pay, it allows compensation. Regarding the statement that a minister is worthy of his wages, it implicitly denies he deserves anything more than bare sustenance.

Option 8: *Jesus forbids the disciples from acquiring greedily but permits them to receive with pure motives.* While similar to the previous option, this proposal offers an ethic of motivation rather than an ethic of moderation. That is, rather than regulating the disciples' external activities, it regulates the desires of their heart. However, nothing in the text substantiates this resolution.

We need a better option. As is typically the case in interpreting Scripture, the key to understanding this passage is found in the context.

The Source of Payment

The primary concern of Matthew 10:8–10 is not *what* is received or *how* it is received but *from whom* it is received. The disciples are *not* to receive from those to whom they minister. They *are* to receive from God. The key to all this is found in the word "laborer."

Both Matthew and Luke speak of a "laborer" being worthy of payment, yet neither author newly introduces this term at this point in their respective gospels. Rather, they appeal to the words of Christ in the preceding passages where he calls for laborers to enter the harvest.

> Then he said to his disciples, "The harvest is plentiful,
> but the laborers are few; therefore pray earnestly to the
> Lord of the harvest to send out laborers into his harvest."
> (Matt. 9:37–38; cf. Luke 10:2)

The employer of the laborers pays their wages. In this metaphor, the employer is "the Lord of the harvest," not the grain. Translating this image to reality, *God* is the employer, not the recipients of the gospel message. While we may be tempted to identify those individuals who provide for the disciples as the employers or clients who pay the wages, they are rather God's instruments in this kingdom economy. The Lord of the harvest commissions his laborers, orchestrating their supply from the grain of the field.

This stands in stark contrast to the idea that in saying "the laborer is worthy of his wages," Jesus calls those who receive the gospel to offer payment to ministers as their employers or clients. Such a conclusion mistakes the grain for God, the harvest for its Lord.

According to their commission, the disciples are not at liberty to give their ministry in return for payment, but in the course of ministry they may receive support that God has furnished at the hands of men. In the words of John Nolland, "… the provision of food… is not thought of as coming from those benefiting from the ministry, which they identify as a worthy ministry; the provision is thought of as being arranged by God (wherever it might come from at a practical level)."[3]

Reciprocity and Colabor

We are farther on our journey toward the truth, but we are still faced with the difficulty of differentiating between payment from men and

---

[3]Nolland, *The Gospel of Matthew*, 418.

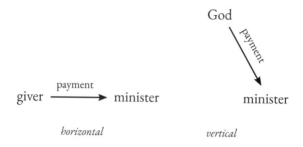

Figure 1.1: Horizontal vs. Vertical Payment

payment from God. Since the disciples receive support at the hands of fellow men and not in packages falling from heaven, how does one begin to distinguish the two? How do we articulate the difference between horizontal payment from man to minister and vertical payment from the Lord of the harvest to his laborer?

The key here is in the notion of *obligation*. In a purely horizontal exchange, a man finds himself obligated to a minister. In a contribution representing a vertical payment from God, some other obligation secures the arrangement. I will call these two sorts of transactions *ministerial reciprocity* and *ministerial colabor*, shortening them simply to *reciprocity* and *colabor*.[4]

Ministerial reciprocity: *Support (material or otherwise) given to a minister out of a sense of direct obligation for his ministry of the gospel.*

The term *reciprocity* describes a contribution offered out of a direct obligation—i.e., one that is not mediated by God. One who gives out of direct obligation considers himself primarily beholden to the one who receives. For example, reciprocity occurs when one gives money to a preacher in exchange for the gospel that was preached.

---

[4]"Colabor" is not a formal English word, but the distinction and frequency with which we will use it warrants coining our own term rather than using the hyphenated "co-labor."

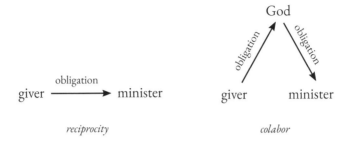

Figure 1.2: Reciprocity vs. Colabor

This notion includes asymmetric exchanges and voluntary exchanges. For example, ministerial reciprocity occurs even when only a pittance is offered and even when no fee is requested, so long as the giver gives from a sense of indebtedness to the minister.

Ministerial colabor: *Support (material or otherwise) given by man to a minister out of a sense of obligation to God, to honor or aid in the proclamation of the gospel.*

Unlike the direct sense of obligation involved in reciprocity, *colabor* acknowledges a mediated obligation, the giver considering himself indebted directly to the Lord, and through that obligation finding himself duty-bound to give to a minister. I call this colabor because it is the product of fellow servants working toward a common goal of a common Employer.

Jesus forbids *ministerial reciprocity* in Matthew 10:8 when he commands his disciples to "give without pay." On the other hand, he permits and even promotes *ministerial colabor* in Matthew 10:9–10 when he instructs the disciples not to bring their own provisions because "the laborer deserves his food." In the chapters ahead, I will refer to this dual ethic as *the dorean principle*, *dorean* being the Greek word in Matthew 10:8 translated as "freely" or "without pay."

The Dorean Principle: *In the context of gospel proclamation, accepting support as anything other than an act of colabor compromises the sincerity of ministry.*

Wages as Colabor

With these definitions in mind, we can move forward to Matthew and Luke and establish that the pattern of support Jesus describes should be regarded as an instance of colabor.

First, the disciples are not to receive money from all who benefit from their ministry but are to restrict themselves to the hospitality of one in each city (Matt. 10:11; Luke 10:7). If they were to gather support more broadly, we might imagine a pattern of ministerial reciprocity. All recipients of ministry would be counted as owing the disciples, and at least the willing ones would be called to compensate them with their resources. However, the selective sources of support indicate that the disciples are not permitted to broadly impose direct obligation on those to whom they minister.

Second, an act of colabor takes place when two servants coordinate their efforts for the sake of a common master, and indeed, those who support the disciples share the same Master. While we may only be able to term them citizens of the kingdom of God anachronistically (cf. Matt. 10:7; Luke 10:9), those who support the disciples are firmly established among God's people. Jesus restricts the disciples from going to Gentile or Samaritan territories (Matt. 10:5), but within each Judean city they visit, they are to find one who is "worthy" (Matt. 10:11–12) and "a son of peace" (Luke 10:6). This vocabulary indicates one who is already qualified to colabor for the good of the coming kingdom. The passages further evidence the expectation of support from the Judean population through an especially strong response to rejection. To pronounce condemnation, the disciples are to shake the dust off their feet (Matt. 10:14; Luke 10:10–11). Thus, Jesus can say it will be better for Sodom and Gomorrah on the day of judgment than for those who have rejected the gospel (Matt. 10:15; Luke 10:1). A parallel command of Christ at the end of Luke further demonstrates this principle of colabor.

> He said to them, "But now let the one who has a money-
> bag take it, and likewise a knapsack. And let the one who
> has no sword sell his cloak and buy one. (Luke 22:36)

Before, the disciples were told that they should take no moneybag because a laborer is worthy of his wages. Now, they are told that they *should* take a moneybag. Certainly, the laborer has not become less worthy. On the night of his betrayal, Jesus modifies his earlier command in order to prepare the disciples for their imminent journey into a hostile environment. Previously, the disciples could venture into new territories and expect to find fellow servants of God ready to colabor with them by providing material support for their mission. From now on, this expectation would be abandoned and replaced with the anticipation of opposition. In the context of this passage, Jesus warns the disciples of the coming persecution at the hands of Jews, but his words apply equally to Gentiles. A people not for Christ is a people against him (Matt. 12:30; Luke 11:23).

However, we should hesitate to conclude that Jesus only sought to address overt hostility. The disciples encountered curious minds more than willing to pay for their services (cf. Acts 8:18). In settings absent of the converted, they found lands potentially ripe for reciprocity but barren for colabor. It seems reasonable to suspect Christ instructed his disciples to carry moneybags not merely because they could not predictively expect support but because they could not even ethically receive it.

Regardless, Jesus's instructions to his disciples in Matthew and Luke fit neatly into a pattern of colabor. They are to receive help from those who offer out of service to a common Master. In offering the gospel, they are not to request a commercial exchange from anyone, especially not from the broad masses they seek to reach.

The Zeal of Christ

Before we move away from the red letters to other parts of the New Testament, I would like to emphasize just how seriously Jesus regarded the intersection of money and ministry. In one particular event—recorded by all four gospel authors—Jesus forcefully chased money changers out from the temple (Matt. 21:12–13; Mark 11:15–17; Luke 19:45–46; John 2:13–17). Clearly, he objected to the misuse of the things of God for the sake of gain, and his disapproval is no small matter. In fact, the disciples recognized this consuming zeal as the fulfillment of Old Testament prophecy (John 2:17).

In this vein, Jesus rejected Satan's propositions of material gain (Matt. 4:3, 9; Luke 4:3). He likewise expects his followers to resist temptation rather than compromise for the sake of wealth. As he himself said, you cannot serve both God and money (Matt. 6:24; Luke 16:13).

Conclusion

The words of Christ are a great treasure. Beginning there, we have found a distinction between *ministerial reciprocity* and *ministerial colabor*. The former establishes a direct obligation between man and minister, and the other mediates that obligation through God, the Lord of the harvest.

Popular theologian D. A. Carson notes a similar scheme in Matthew 10:8–10, remarking that while "the service rendered must not be bought or sold," a church has the duty to provide for its ministers.[5] He further observes, "This particular arrangement continues, I would be prepared to argue, in the letters of Paul …."[6] This leads us to another treasure: the writings of the apostle.

---

[5]Carson, *When Jesus Confronts the World*, 142.
[6]Ibid., 142.

2

The Policy of Paul

Contradiction vs. Consistency

I have known many who express a fondness for the TV series *NCIS*. Although I have never watched a full episode, I have enjoyed several clips from the show featuring hacking scenes. In the most fantastic of them all, two characters attempt to stop a hacker who has gained access to their computer, an act which for some reason manifests as a series of pop-up windows appearing on the screen. To work as quickly as possible, both heroes type on the keyboard at the same time, scanning through lines of source code that intermittently appear on the screen. However, the hacker is finally stopped by a third hero who, in an act of common sense genius, thinks to unplug the monitor. From personal and professional experience, let me tell you that computer security does not even remotely work this way.

From blunders like this come the phrase "write what you know." That is, the best kind of writing originates from some author who shares real experience in the subject matter. It is unlikely the creators of *NCIS* had any deep background in computing.

Unlike some, the apostle Paul was a man who wrote about what he knew. Being personally trained by Gamaliel (a master of the Jewish religion) and Jesus (*the* Master of Christianity), Paul knew much of faith in God and the doctrines he expounded in his epistles. This was no less the case when it came to ministry fundraising. In this arena,

Paul had experienced more than any of Jesus's early disciples. The most prolific among the apostles, Paul incurred sizable financial needs. One scholar has estimated that even the production of an epistle like Romans would cost $2,275 in present-day dollars.[1] Naturally, Paul must have frequently contemplated the flow of money in gospel labors.

If you have not previously investigated the matter of ministry fundraising, the frequency with which Paul addresses the topic may astound you. While Paul addresses some other topics of weighty significance rarely—for example, the Lord's supper—he frequently makes mention of fundraising practices. Beyond those texts regarding the collection for the poor in Jerusalem, major pericopae include the entirety of 1 Corinthians 9, 2 Corinthians 11:1–15, 1 Thessalonians 2:9–12, 2 Thessalonians 3:6–12, and Philippians 4:10–20. There is no shortage of Pauline passages that have some bearing on ministry finance.

At the same time, an initial look at Paul's ministry may cause us to level charges of inconsistency. He commands people to give to ministers, yet rejects their attempts at payment. Sometimes he even receives money from the same people he earlier refused. Does he arbitrarily create rules the way *NCIS* arbitrarily creates fictional security threats?

In this chapter, I want to take a look at the Corinthian epistles, where the apostle most directly sets forward his financial policy. We will see that Paul is perfectly consistent, adopting the exact same pattern Jesus set for his disciples.

Rejection of Reciprocity

In 1 Corinthians 9 and 2 Corinthians 11, Paul explains that he refuses to preach for pay. He lists a variety of reasons *why* he does this, but these reasons may not overturn the simple *what* of his actions. In both of these passages, the apostle provides a direct description of his policy: to *preach the gospel free of charge.*

---

[1] Richards, *Paul and First-Century Letter Writing*, 169.

> What then is my reward? That in my preaching I may present the gospel free of charge, so as not to make full use of my right in the gospel. (1 Cor. 9:18)

> Or did I commit a sin in humbling myself so that you might be exalted, because I preached God's gospel to you free of charge? (2 Cor. 11:7)

Simply stated, Paul rejects reciprocity, all that is offered in direct exchange for his work of ministry.

Many assume that Paul refuses Corinthian funds to preserve his independence.[2] By accepting their money, he would implicitly grant them the status of patron, obligating himself to them. However, as frequently as this motivation is assumed, Paul never intimates it. Further, a host of problems prohibit this understanding,[3] not the least of which is that Paul's epistles do not indicate that the Corinthians seek to have some status over Paul, but that they seek to have some status *under* him. That is, if the patronage model should be applied, the Corinthians wish to be Paul's clients, not his patrons. Instead, we must look elsewhere to elucidate the apostle's rationale.

Reception of *Propempo* Support

Despite his commitments, the apostle Paul does not reject financial support altogether, even in the context of his gospel preaching. For example, in both Corinthian epistles, he speaks of his intentions to come to Corinth in order to be sent by them to Macedonia.

> I will visit you after passing through Macedonia, for I intend to pass through Macedonia, and perhaps I will stay with you or even spend the winter, so that you may help me on my journey, wherever I go. (1 Cor. 16:5–6)

> I wanted to visit you on my way to Macedonia, and to come back to you from Macedonia and have you send me on my way to Judea. (2 Cor. 1:16)

---

[2] This patronage hypothesis is the predominant explanation of Paul's policy. See Briones, *Paul's Financial Policy*, 1,169,180,207.

[3] Ibid., 17–18.

The word for "help" and "send" in these verses is the Greek word *propempo*, a term with financial overtones, meaning "to assist someone in making a journey, send on one's way with food, money, by arranging for companions, means of travel, etc."[4] For example, when Paul commands Titus to *propempo* Zenas and Apollos, he is to do so "seeing that they lack nothing" (Titus 3:13).

In each of these verses, Paul makes it clear that he intends to have the Corinthians support him in his missionary travels. In 1 Corinthians 16:6–7, the anticipation of an extended stay focuses on the Corinthians helping the apostle rather than the apostle ministering to them. Additionally, rather than referring to the blessing of Paul's ministry, the "second experience of grace" in 2 Cor. 1:15 likely refers to the Corinthians' opportunity to support the apostle.[5] This fits with Paul's use of "grace" to refer to generosity and service (1 Cor. 16:3; 2 Cor. 8:4, 6–7, 19). Yet how does this anticipation of *propempo* support fit with Paul's stated commitment to refuse any payment from the Corinthians?

Propempo as Colabor

If Paul permanently refuses Corinthian support, yet also plans to accept it, there is an apparent contradiction. However, we can resolve this discrepancy by recognizing that while Paul resolutely opposes the reciprocity of Corinthian payment, *propempo* support more naturally falls under the rubric of colabor.

Consider some of the biblical uses of the term:

- The church of Antioch sent (*propempo*'d) Paul and Barnabas to the Jerusalem council in order to deal with the threat of the Judaizers (Acts 15:3). That is, the Antiochians colabored with Paul and Barnabas to defend the gospel.

- Paul asks to be sent (*propempo*'d) to Spain by the Roman church (Rom. 15:24), presumably for the purpose of evangelism. In

---

[4] Bauer, *A Greek-English Lexicon of the New Testament and Other Early Christian Literature, Third Edition*, 837.

[5] Fee, "ΧΑΡΙΣ in II Corinthians I.15."

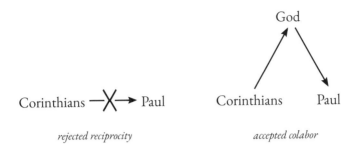

Figure 2.1: Paul and Corinthian Funds

other words, he asks them to colabor with him for the propagation of the gospel.

- Paul requests *propempo* support for Timothy on the grounds that "he is doing the work of the Lord, as I am" (1 Cor. 16:10–11). The Corinthians are to assist—or colabor—with Timothy in this work.

- Paul likewise solicits *propempo* support for Zenas and Apollos. While Zenas is otherwise unknown, Apollos undoubtedly performs some ministerial work that Titus—and presumably, his congregation—is to help with by sending them on their way (Titus 3:13). They are to colabor with Zenas and Apollos to promote the teaching of the gospel.

- In perhaps the clearest instance of colabor, John argues that Gaius should send out (*propempo*) noble missionaries "that we may be fellow workers for the truth" (3 John 8).

So is *propempo* support colabor? Plainly. By sending Paul on his way, the Corinthians would assist him in proclaiming the gospel in Macedonia or any other destination. In fact, in the very same context, he calls himself a colaborer (2 Cor. 1:24).

Paul does not reject all money but only that which would constitute payment and compromise his free-of-charge proclamation of the gospel. Thus, Paul can say that he does not write to receive "any such provision" (i.e., reciprocity) in 1 Corinthians 9:15, while also writing to receive some provision as he is sent out on his way (i.e., colabor) in 1 Corinthians 16:5–6.

Labor as Suffering

If the idea of treating money as colabor seems odd, we should start by first looking at Paul's view of labor and how it relates to suffering. Labor and suffering may seem like disparate concepts, but consider how frequently Paul lists toil among his many persecutions.

> To the present hour we hunger and thirst, we are poorly dressed and buffeted and homeless, and *we labor, working with our own hands*. (1 Cor. 4:11–12)

> … but as servants of God we commend ourselves in every way: by great endurance, in afflictions, hardships, calamities, beatings, imprisonments, riots, *labors*, sleepless nights, hunger; … (1 Cor. 6:4–5)

> Are they servants of Christ? I am a better one—I am talking like a madman—with *far greater labors*, far more imprisonments, with countless beatings, and often near death. Five times I received at the hands of the Jews the forty lashes less one. Three times I was beaten with rods. Once I was stoned. Three times I was shipwrecked; a night and a day I was adrift at sea; on frequent journeys, in danger from rivers, danger from robbers, danger from my own people, danger from Gentiles, danger in the city, danger in the wilderness, danger at sea, danger from false brothers; *in toil and hardship*, through many a sleepless night, in hunger and thirst, often without food, in cold and exposure. (2 Cor. 11:24–27)

Paul does not distinguish between manual labor and all the other forms of hardship he endures for the sake of the gospel. In waiving the financial returns of secular toil in order to fund his own ministry, he suffers. This truth extends to all people: Any who work, denying themselves the fruit of their labor, suffer.

Colabor as Shared Suffering

If *labor* is suffering, then *ministerial colabor* is nothing more than shared suffering for the sake of the gospel. This becomes apparent in Galatians, where Paul speaks of giving to ministers in the context of carrying each other's burdens.[6]

> Bear one another's burdens, and so fulfill the law of Christ. … Let the one who is taught the word share all good things with the one who teaches. (Gal. 6:2, 6)

Those who sacrificially give in order to spare Paul the task of secular employment suffer hand in hand with him, carrying a portion of his burdens. When one gives for the sake of the gospel, he experiences self-imposed hardship (e.g., financial loss) in order to bolster the efforts of another who voluntarily experiences hardship directly in the mission field. As the book of Hebrews declares, to help one who is persecuted is to join in that experience of persecution (Heb. 10:33).

Those that give to the apostle do not simply labor *with* him but also in the employment of the same Master. Paul continues to explain that one who gives to a minister ultimately gives to God.

> Do not be deceived: God is not mocked, for whatever one sows, that will he also reap. For the one who sows to his own flesh will from the flesh reap corruption, but the one who sows to the Spirit will from the Spirit reap eternal life. (Gal. 6:7–8)

Paul considers one who gives for the sake of the gospel as sowing to the Spirit. That is, in this spiritual economy, the direct and ultimate obligation is to God rather than the minister. Note that "the Spirit" in this context refers to the Holy Spirit (cf. Gal. 5:16–25).

---

[6]While it does not appear in all English versions, Paul introduces v. 6 with a connective word, often translated as "now," that joins vv. 1–5 to vv. 6–10.

Acts of giving and hospitality are colabor in the fullest sense. For a minister's needs to be met, either he or other believers must engage in some profit-generating enterprise to fund his ministry. Regardless of who performs the work, that secular labor supports the same spiritual ministry.

The Blessing of Shared Suffering

The apostle Paul has no qualms with others experiencing this hardship for the sake of the gospel because while they suffer together, they receive comfort together.

> Our hope for you is unshaken, for we know that as you share in our sufferings, you will also share in our comfort. (2 Cor. 1:7)

On the other hand, reciprocity lacks any similar spiritual benefit. One who gives out of a sense of duty to man does not experience suffering in service to God.

This explains how Paul can simultaneously refuse and receive support in differing contexts. Furthermore, it explains how he can simultaneously reject funds and command his churches to support the work of ministry (cf. 1 Cor. 9:14; Gal. 6:6). By declining payment, he does not prevent anyone from fulfilling their obligation to give but frees them to do so rightly in order that they might be truly blessed.

Conclusion

Do you see the connection to our discoveries in the previous chapter? Paul's policy follows the command of Christ. In refusing ministerial reciprocity while accepting—and encouraging—ministerial colabor, Paul does precisely what Jesus commanded of his disciples. In fact, both Jesus and Paul use the same Greek word (*dorean*) to describe their ministry as being "free of charge" (2 Cor. 11:7; Matt. 10:8).

While initially perplexing, Paul's behavior is perfectly consistent. His fidelity to the dorean principle leads him to reject direct payment for the gospel, yet otherwise accept assistance. Duty to God must triumph over a sensed debt to any minister since God mediates all obligation to his servants as ministers. In the next chapter, we will consider the nature and shape of this mediated obligation as we continue to examine 1 Corinthians 9.

3

The Triangle of Obligation

Immediacy vs. Indirection

I was 23 years old and had never met my *lolo* (that's the Tagalog word for grandfather). Several factors, including the untimely death of my mother—his daughter—as well as his roots in the Philippines left us distant and without common ties. Driving a stereo-less Honda Accord and armed with the return address on a letter I had received 12 years prior, I set off on a 2,400-mile road trip with the hope of connecting with him. The overall journey had a larger purpose—I was moving from Virginia to California—but this was an essential side quest. As I investigated the neighborhood, I discovered the house had belonged to his sister. Some of the neighbors were still in touch with her, and she was able to get me in touch with him. He only visited the United States a few weeks a year, and by God's providence, it just so happened that he would be arriving shortly.

When the time came, I was equipped with a new address and headed off to meet my lolo. It was a sweet reunion, if first-time meetings between relatives may be called reunions. I had the privilege of not only meeting him but several other relatives as well, including his oldest son, my uncle, Tito Gie. Tito Gie's hospitality was fantastic. He housed me for several days, and hardly a moment passed where food was not being prepared or offered to me. In part, this is par for the course in Filipino homes, but as I spoke with him, I learned that he felt the need to treat me well in order to honor my mother, the sister he had never met. Needless to say, that weekend remains one of the most memorable in my life.

Tito Gie considered himself obligated to me but only indirectly so. Rather than an immediate or direct indebtedness, his felt obligation toward me was mediated through my late mother. Visually, we might picture this as a triangle.

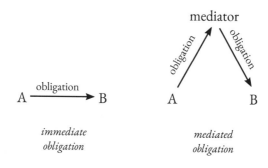

Figure 3.1: Immediate vs. Mediated Obligation

In the first two chapters, we saw that both Jesus and Paul forbid receiving ministerial support out of a direct obligation (reciprocity) but encourage support that arises out of a mediated obligation (co-labor). This ethic—the dorean principle—fits into the same sort of triangle.[1]

I would like to use that notion of mediated obligation as a lens through which we will examine a broader collection of examples. Specifically, in 1 Corinthians 9, Paul reinforces this principle of co-labor through several analogies to ministry fundraising. Let's take a look at these and see how this pattern takes shape.

---

[1] This notion of a triangle is inspired by David E. Briones's work, *Paul's Financial Policy: A Socio-Theological Approach*. See Owens, "Divine Mediation in Paul's Financial Policy."

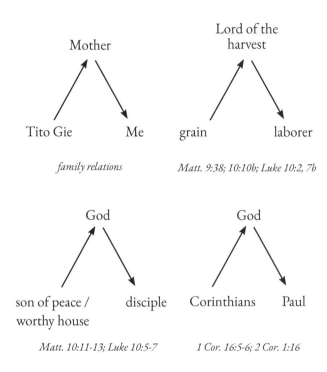

Figure 3.2: Examples of Mediated Obligation

The Priesthood

The last analogy that Paul employs is in many ways the most direct of the lot. According to the apostle, the general principles of ministerial maintenance in Old Testament Israel must carry over into the New Testament church.

> Do you not know that those who are employed in the temple service get their food from the temple, and those who serve at the altar share in the sacrificial offerings? In the same way, the Lord commanded that those who proclaim the gospel should get their living by the gospel. (1 Cor. 9:13–14)

Paul appeals to the pattern established by the Levitical priesthood. While we have started our investigation of ministers and money with the words of Christ and the acts of Paul, this will take us back to the earliest pages of the Bible to see how God provided for his laborers.

The law of Moses specifies that the Levites receive the food from the Lord's food offering (Num. 18:8–20; Deut. 18:1–5); everything contributed but not burned becomes the possession of the sons of Aaron (Lev. 2:1–3; 7:33–35). Similar to the contributions of food offerings, this same book of law records the right of the Levites to the tithes, composed of the produce of the land and other valuable materials (Num. 18:21–24). While the tribe as a whole only nominally inherits the food offerings, the tithes are in fact shared this broadly.

On one hand, it appears that this transaction between the citizens at large and the priestly tribe constitutes an expression of obligation of the people of Israel to the Levites. It is repeatedly termed a "perpetual due" from the former party to the latter (Num. 18:8, 11, 19) and in practical terms, this due is given directly to the priests (Deut. 18:3).

However, the transaction is not primarily horizontal as may be easily recognized from its designation as an offering to the Lord. In the passages cited above, the sacrifices are called "the contributions made to me [the Lord]" (Num. 18:8) and "the LORD's food offerings" (Deut. 18:1). The Lord likewise labels the tithes "a contribution to the Lord" (Num. 18:24). While the tithes and offerings are given *to* the Lord, the book of Numbers also says they are given *by* the Lord (Num. 18:8, 12, 19, 21, 24). These two primary directions of flow must control our understanding of the secondary direction of flow. The Israelites give to the Levites, but more importantly, the Israelites give to God who in turn gives to the Levites. After all, we would not imagine the people of Israel making their sacrifices to mere men. To speak of resources passing from man to man simply abbreviates the larger transaction. As the Lord says to the Levites in Numbers 18:12, "the firstfruits of what they give to the LORD, I give to you."

Note that the express significance of the phrase "the LORD is their inheritance" resides in this arrangement between the Levites and their Israelite brothers (Num. 18:20; cf. Deut. 18:1–2). On one hand, this simply acknowledges what we have already identified: the Lord

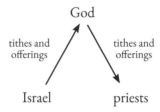

Verse	Given to God	Given by God
8a	contributions made to me	I have given you charge
8b	all the consecrated things	I have given them to you
9	which they render to me	shall be yours
11	the contribution of their gift	I have given them to you
12	what they give to the Lord	I give to you
13	which they bring to the Lord	shall be yours
14	Every devoted thing	shall be yours
15	which they offer to the Lord	shall be yours
19	contributions… to the Lord	I give to you
21	every tithe	To the Levites, I have given
24	a contribution to the Lord	I have given to the Levites

Figure 3.3: The Triangle of Obligation in Numbers 18

provides for the Levites. On another hand, it shows the exclusivity of this mode of support. It is not merely that the Levites are to have the Lord as an inheritance, receiving from the contributions, but they are to have no other inheritance. The law of Moses permits the priests to receive colabor, that which is offered to the Lord, but forbids reciprocity. Consequently, in Israel's times of faithlessness—i.e., when they do not colabor—the Levites languish (cf. Deut. 14:27; Neh. 13:10). Perhaps the Levites may find other means of sustaining themselves, but in the context of their ministry, the Levites forfeit the typical modes of sustenance enjoyed by other tribes. For the sake of the divine blessing, they do not engage in property accrual, and they do not exchange their services for payment.

When this model is violated and a priest accepts offerings directly, he essentially puts himself in the place of God. As a divinely appointed broker, he disseminates the Lord's blessings through the work of ministry but then robs from the Lord what is owed in return. Such was the sin of Hophni and Phinehas, the corrupt sons of Samuel who took raw meat before it had been offered to the Lord (1 Sam. 2:12–17).

This model keenly foreshadows the tensions and resolutions we have seen in the gospels. Jesus forbids payment for ministry (reciprocity) but insists that workers are to receive from other members of the kingdom as wages from God (colabor).

Paul's Metaphors

In addition to his reference to the Levitical priesthood, Paul makes several other analogies that exhibit the same pattern of mediated obligation.

> Who serves as a soldier at his own expense? Who plants a vineyard without eating any of its fruit? Or who tends a flock without getting some of the milk? Do I say these things on human authority? Does not the Law say the same? For it is written in the Law of Moses, "You shall not muzzle an ox when it treads out the grain." Is it for oxen that God is concerned? Does he not certainly speak for our sake? It was written for our sake, because the plowman should plow in hope and the thresher thresh in hope of sharing in the crop. (1 Cor. 9:7–10)

While an initial reading may lead one to imagine Paul describing a direct obligation between man and minister, a brief contemplation of his various metaphors reveal that, in each case, the obligation is mediated. In each, the one who gives is not the employer who contractually pays but simply the source of material provision used to supply the laborer. In each, the one who gives is not primarily obligated to the laborer but to the laborer's employer.

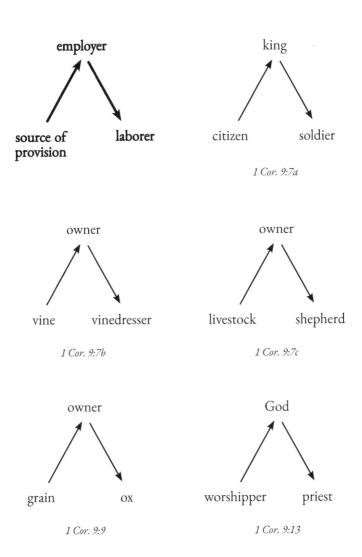

Figure 3.4: The Triangle of Obligation in 1 Corinthians 9

The vine does not supply out of obligation to the vinedresser, and the citizen does not supply out of obligation to the soldier. The former supplies out of obligation to the owner and the latter out of obligation to the king. Representing the Lord, the owner and the king ultimately reward the laborer by assorted means of provision. Likewise, the laborer commissioned by God does not ultimately receive his pay from those to whom he ministers, even if he receives it at their hands. His just reward is granted by God through human means. His just reward is granted through colabor, not reciprocity.

Widows

This passage leads us to another parallel: the church's provision for widows. The connection may not be immediately obvious, but in 1 Timothy 5, Paul once again cites the ox in the law of Moses along with the words of Christ in order to illustrate the nature of the church's obligation to its ministers.

> Let the elders who rule well be considered worthy of double honor, especially those who labor in preaching and teaching. For the Scripture says, "You shall not muzzle an ox when it treads out the grain," and, "The laborer deserves his wages." (1 Tim. 5:17–18)

In the New Testament, the term "honor" (*time*, in Greek) frequently denotes "price" or "value" (cf. Matt. 27:6–9; Acts 4:34; 5:2–3), as in English, where we speak of the "honorarium" paid to a speaker. Some take this injunction of double honor to mean that those elders who preach and teach should receive double the pay received by other elders. However, notice that the verse says no such thing. Rather, it says that *all* elders who rule well should be counted worthy of double honor. Those who preach and teach are simply exemplars among this single group.

So if the term "double" does not imply a comparison between teaching and non-teaching elders, what does it compare? The key to this is found earlier in the chapter, where Paul commands that another demographic in the church receive honor.[2]

> Honor widows who are truly widows. … Let a widow be enrolled if she is not less than sixty years of age, having been the wife of one husband, and having a reputation for good works: if she has brought up children, has shown hospitality, has washed the feet of the saints, has cared for the afflicted, and has devoted herself to every good work. (1 Tim. 5:3, 9–10)

Paul instructs Timothy to "honor" (*timao*, in Greek), the widows. That is, he should enroll them in some program where they will receive regular financial support in correlation with their service to the church. However, one would not imagine that the widows are being paid in direct exchange for their works. If this were the case, the exclusion of widows with families would be unjust (1 Tim. 5:4). Rather, in their need, they are to be honored as servants of God by less needy servants of God. That is, the church does not find itself directly obligated to the widows for their service—otherwise, they would pay all widows—but finds itself obligated to God who commands his neediest servants be spared the shame of destitution.

Given that Paul relates the honoring of widows to the honoring of elders, this triangle of obligation must shape our understanding of how church leaders are to be compensated. The notion of colabor present in the support of widows must be present in the support of elders.

Jerusalem

Back in 1 Corinthians 9, between the Levitical priesthood and the other six analogies, Paul makes the following comment:

> If we have sown spiritual things among you, is it too much if we reap material things from you? (1 Cor. 9:11)

---

[2]For a fuller discussion, see Waldron, "A Careful Exposition of 1 Timothy 5:17," 76–84.

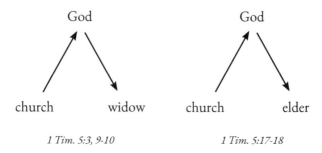

Figure 3.5: The Triangle of Obligation in 1 Timothy 5

This bears remarkable similarity to something the apostle says regarding the Jerusalem collection, a financial collection among Gentile churches for the poor in Jerusalem.

> For [the Gentile churches] were pleased to do it, and indeed they owe it to [the church in Jerusalem]. For if the Gentiles have come to share in their spiritual blessings, they ought also to be of service to them in material blessings. (Rom. 15:27)

By using the same language to discuss these issues, Paul frames the Jerusalem collection as a matter of ministerial support. This leaves us with one more analogous triangle to examine.

Paul regards the Gentiles as debtors who owe the Jews, yet he treats the collection as an act of worship,[3] demonstrating a mediated obligation, owed primarily to God. For example, he orders that people gather for this offering on the Christian day of worship, the first day of the week (1 Cor. 16:2). Furthermore, he describes the offering with vocabulary (Greek, *leitourgia*) that indicates a religious service (2 Cor. 9:12; Rom. 15:27). In fact, in 2 Corinthians, offering a primary motivation for participation in the collection, Paul points to the Father's gift of the Son and the Son's willing sacrifice of his life (2 Cor. 8:9; cf. 9:13,

---

[3]See Downs, *The Offering of the Gentiles*, 120–160.

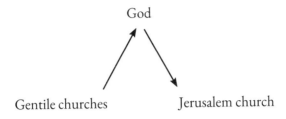

Figure 3.6: The Triangle of Obligation in Romans 15

15). In other words, the Gentiles owe this gift to the Lord and are to offer it by sharing it with his needy servants. It is a religious sacrifice rendered to God rather than to the Jews, just as it generates thanks to God rather than to the Gentiles (2 Cor. 9:11–12).

There exists a real obligation here between Gentile and Jew, but the Lord mediates that obligation. The Gentiles do not give payment to the Jews for services performed, but offer colabor, a mutual facilitation of kingdom sustenance.

Conclusion

In 1 Corinthians 9, Paul confirms the pattern of mediated obligation that we saw in the first two chapters. Through various analogies of nature and society, he unmistakably replicates this triangle. Additionally, he draws the analogy more directly when he illustrates the nature of this obligation with the Levitical priesthood and the church in Jerusalem.

In the next chapter, we will see how Paul addresses the importance of this mediated obligation with his use of the term *burden*. However, if at this point you are eager to learn more about practical application of the dorean principle, feel free to look through Chapters 11–14 before continuing.

4

The Burden of Support

Difficulty vs. Obligation

I've always enjoyed telling riddles; it's one of my favorite pastimes. Others might inform you that I enjoy "torturing people with" riddles. Once I've stated the enigma, I refuse to give hints beyond answers to "yes" or "no" questions.

Whenever a brave soul agrees to this experience, the first riddle I usually tell goes like this: "Joe is afraid to go home because the man with the mask is there. Where is Joe?" I'd prefer to let you struggle to determine the answer through carefully thought-out questions, but despite advances in technology, I cannot do that through this book. I will just have to tell you the answer: "third base." Joe is a baseball player afraid of stealing home base because the masked catcher protects the plate.

The fun of this particular riddle lies in the fact that the hearer typically imagines a scene from a horror movie. What hidden villain awaits Joe at his house? Usually, it isn't until the end of the process that the riddle solver begins to reorient his thinking around other scenarios such as sports.

Similar to the diversion of this riddle, when Paul speaks of burdening his churches through ministry fundraising, people often assume his concern revolves around the notion of imposed difficulty. He does not accept money because he wishes to avoid placing undue hardships on anyone. However, our investigation from the previous chapter and the various triangle diagrams we developed should lead us to wonder whether he instead speaks of imposed obligation.

In this chapter, we will examine how Paul uses the notion of "burden" to describe his financial disposition toward three churches: the church of Philippi, the church of Thessalonica, and the church of Corinth. As we do, we will see that Paul's mentions of "burden" do not primarily refer to difficulty but to a direct obligation between man and minister that contends with an obligation mediated by God.

Corinth and Thessalonica

Paul occasionally uses the word "burden" to explain his refusal of funds from the Corinthians and Thessalonians.[1]

> For in what were you less favored than the rest of the churches, except that I myself did not **burden** you? Forgive me this wrong! Here for the third time I am ready to come to you. And I will not be a **burden**, for I seek not what is yours but you. For children are not obligated to save up for their parents, but parents for their children. (2 Cor. 12:13–14)

> For you remember, brothers, our labor and toil: we worked night and day, that we might not be a **burden** to any of you, while we proclaimed to you the gospel of God. (1 Thess. 2:9)

> For you yourselves know how you ought to imitate us, because we were not idle when we were with you, nor did we eat anyone's bread without paying for it, but with toil and labor we worked night and day, that we might not be a **burden** to any of you. (2 Thess. 3:7–8)

Specifically, Paul claims that his refusal of Corinthian and Thessalonian support stems from his unwillingness to burden them. A

---

[1] More precisely, Paul alternates between two root words in Greek—*narkao* and *bareo*—to communicate the notion of "burden."

common understanding of these verses says that Paul does not wish to impose undue hardship on these churches. Certainly, the word "burden" frequently emphasizes difficulty, but the picture complexifies when set in contrast to the apostle's disposition toward the church of Philippi.

Philippi

Writing to the Corinthians, Paul hyperbolically claims that he has robbed the churches of Macedonia in order to avoid burdening them.

> I robbed other churches by accepting support from them in order to serve you. And when I was with you and was in need, I did not burden anyone, for the brothers who came from Macedonia supplied my need. So I refrained and will refrain from **burdening** you in any way. (2 Cor. 11:8–9)

In writing to the church in Philippi—the most prominent church in Macedonia—Paul confirms that no others supported him.[2]

> And you Philippians yourselves know that in the beginning of the gospel, when I left Macedonia, no church entered into partnership with me in giving and receiving, except you only. (Phil. 4:15)

Another hint that Paul received Philippian aid appears in Acts when Silas and Timothy join him from Macedonia. Though Paul had been working as a tent-maker (Acts 18:3) and reasoning from Scripture only on the Sabbath (Acts 18:4), he began to preach full-time when they arrived (Acts 18:5). This seems to imply that Paul's companions arrive with finances from Macedonia so that he no longer needs to work.[3] Not only in Corinth but also in Thessalonica, Paul receives aid from Philippi (Phil. 2:25; 4:16–18). So why this disparity between Philippi and Corinth/Thessalonica?

---

[2]Paul says he robbed "churches" (2 Cor. 11:8) but that only Philippi supported him (Phil. 4:15). It is possible there may have been multiple churches in Philippi. See Briones, *Paul's Financial Policy*.

[3]So Verbrugge and Krell, *Paul and Money*, 71.

Burden as Difficulty

If we entertain the idea that Paul does not wish to impose undue hardship, then we might conclude the churches of Corinth and Thessalonica are impoverished compared to the church in Philippi. This position is, however, untenable.

Nothing suggests uniform poverty among the Corinthians. Instead, we see that they were "mixed socially."[4] When Paul says that not many are of noble birth (1 Cor. 1:26), he implies that some are.[5] Additionally, we see that there are some who are well off (1 Cor. 11:21). The Mediterranean area as a whole economically boomed during the first century.[6]

Philippi, on the other hand, evidences more signs of poverty. Paul describes the Philippians as giving beyond their means (2 Cor. 8:4), and Paul goes as far as to describe it as "robbery" to take money from them (2 Cor. 11:8). If either the church in Corinth or Philippi could be charged with penury, it would be the Philippian church.

More importantly, with his repeated emphasis on sacrificial giving, the apostle seems to have no prohibition on receiving funds from those who would find it economically difficult to give. As we have already seen, he repeatedly expresses a willingness to receive financially from the Corinthians in the form of *propempo* support, yet considers this no undue hardship. The notion of "burden," then, must indicate something other than difficulty.

Burden as Obligation

In each instance where Paul expresses an unwillingness to burden the Corinthians or Thessalonians, he refers to the act of receiving support particularly in the context of initial ministry. After he speaks of his labor to avoid burdening the Thessalonians, the apostle describes himself as a father of young children (1 Thess. 2:11) and a nursing

---

[4] Theissen, *Fortress Introduction to the New Testament*, 75.

[5] See Theissen, "Social Stratification in the Corinthian Community," 72; cf. Origen, "Against Celsus," 3.48.

[6] See Theissen, "Legitimation and Subsistence," 36.

mother (1 Thess. 2:7). This language of immaturity indicates the Thessalonians' initial conversion in contrast to their existence as an established church. Undoubtedly, Paul refers to the same incident when he mentions burdens in 2 Thessalonians 3:8. Paul also speaks of the Corinthians as his children, but more importantly, he recalls how the signs of an apostle were performed when he first avoided burdening the Corinthians (2 Cor. 12:12–13). This, presumably, refers to his initial arrival.

On the other hand, Paul never considers it a burden when he accepts money from firmly established churches. He does not say that he burdened other churches so that he would not burden the Corinthians, but that he did not burden anyone at all (2 Cor. 11:9). In other words, his reception of money from the more established Philippian church does not count as a burden, even though he "robbed" them (2 Cor. 11:8). On its face, 2 Corinthians 12:13 may suggest otherwise ("For in what were you less favored than the rest of the churches, except that I myself did not burden you?"). But the irony present in the verse more likely only indicates that his non-burdensome actions toward other churches would count as burdens if applied to the Corinthians. Besides, it would be difficult to justify the apostle's behavior if he actually did treat his congregations with partiality (cf. James 2:1).

But why does it matter that circumstances of initial ministry correlate to Paul's concern? Quite simply, new converts are likely to offer money in exchange for the gospel. Thus, Paul tells the Corinthians that if he were to accept their offer, his preaching would no longer be free of charge.[7] One who pays for ministry incurs burden because the whole notion of payment presumes some sort of debt, something that is owed.

In other words, Paul uses the word "burden" to refer to the direct obligation imposed by ministerial reciprocity. This becomes more apparent in another verse where he uses one of the same Greek roots (*baros*) to speak of "demands."

> Nor did we seek glory from people, whether from you

---

[7]Notably, Briones agrees that "their money is a *return* for the *initial* gift of the gospel." Briones, *Paul's Financial Policy*, 201.

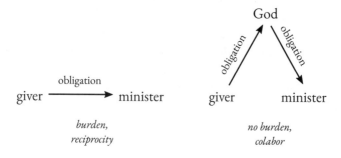

Figure 4.1: Burdensome Giving vs. Burdenless Giving

or from others, though we could have made demands as apostles of Christ. (1 Thess. 2:6)

To be clear, Paul does not employ some special protocol to reject money on initial visits and accept it on others. Neither does he reject money while he is with a congregation and accept it while he is away. On the contrary, he willingly receives from the first Philippian he evangelizes (Acts 16:15; cf. Phil. 1:5), and he indefinitely continues to reject the Corinthians' gift (1 Cor. 9:15; 2 Cor. 11:12). He rejects support most frequently in the context of initial visits, but that is because reciprocity is most frequently offered in the context of an initial visit. The apostle only receives support as colabor, and when he arrives in an unevangelized area, there are rarely colaborers to be found.

Philippian Partnership

In contrast to the passages we have examined regarding the Corinthians and Thessalonians, Paul willingly receives from the Philippians. As you might guess, rather than reciprocity, their offerings of material support constitute colabor.

Paul especially evidences this colabor by his use of the Greek word *koinonia*, often translated as "fellowship" or "partnership." *Koinonia* frequently refers to functional partnerships rather than merely the mutual trust that corresponds to such partnerships. For example, Luke uses it to speak of a business cooperative between fishermen (Luke 5:10).[8] So when the apostle repeats this word in his epistle to the Philippians, describing their mutual relationship, the concept of a joint business venture should color our understanding of their contribution.

Additionally, the "unparalleled"[9] commercial terms used in Philippians 4:10–20 indicate that the Philippians do not offer a gift to Paul so much as a shared resource for achieving gospel-oriented purposes. In other words, they operate as investors, funding a skilled laborer in a common enterprise. Since they both aim for the promotion of the gospel, their transaction does not imply a direct obligation to Paul and thus is not characterized by necessity or by proportional exchange. Those who share the same Lord organically work together to pursue the same goals.

Notably, Julien M. Ogereau—in what is likely the most advanced study on the relationship between Paul and the Philippians—reaches the same conclusions. Regarding the mutuality of the relationship, he writes that rather than exchanging finances/goods/services, Paul and the Philippians contribute to a "common fund,"[10] and that in this model, the contributions "need not have been of equal amount or of similar kind."[11] In other words, the typical quid pro quo exchange of reciprocity is absent. Rather, Paul and the Philippians labor together, the Philippians supplying venture capital and Paul supplying skill, time, and energy.

This resolves an additional mystery about the book of Philippians: why the "thankless thanks?"[12] That is, Paul writes this letter on the

---

[8] See González, "New Testament Koinónia and Wealth," 216,216n40. Elsewhere, Gonzalez argues that this commercial understanding of the term not only pervades the New Testament but also endures among the early church fathers. Gonzalez, *Faith and Wealth*, 71–130.

[9] Sampley, *Pauline Partnership in Christ*, 53.

[10] Ogereau, *Paul's Koinonia with the Philippians*, 289,311.

[11] Ibid., 336.

[12] This is a label that has existed since at least the late nineteenth century. See Pe-

occasion of receiving aid from the Philippians while imprisoned (Phil. 1:14; 4:10), yet not until the very end of the epistle does he directly acknowledge their contribution (Phil. 4:10–20). Even then, rather than highlighting the blessing it is to him personally, he emphasizes his sufficiency without it (Phil. 4:11–13). The notion of colabor illuminates the apostle's otherwise unexpected behavior. The epistle lacks the typical gratitude of a thank you letter because rather than giving to Paul, the Philippians give primarily to God. The apostle commends them for their faithfulness in the matter of his poverty, but their shared purpose is greater than his own well-being. In the words of David E. Briones:

> Recipients merely pass on the commodity of another as mediators or mutual brokers. In this way, both mediating parties equally share a vertical tie of obligation to God, which partly (though not completely) disentangles the horizontal ties of obligation to each other. Put simply, because of the divine third party, obligation ceases to be primarily between Paul and the Philippians.[13]

Briones reckons Paul and the Philippians as mediating parties exchanging resources—gifts originating from God being given to one at the hands of the other—but tacitly identifies God as mediating the obligation between the two.[14]

Paul's description of the Philippians' gift as a sacrifice solidifies this mediated obligation.

> I have received full payment, and more. I am well supplied, having received from Epaphroditus the gifts you sent, a fragrant offering, a sacrifice acceptable and pleasing to God. (Phil. 4:18)

While the Philippians render material support ultimately to Paul, the religious term "sacrifice" indicates that—in a more immediate

---

terman, "'Thankless Thanks': The Epistolary Social Convention In Philippians 4:10–20," 261n2.

[13] Briones, *Paul's Financial Policy*, 120.

[14] See also ibid., 122–128; Briones, "Paul's Intentional 'Thankless Thanks' in Philippians 4.10–20."

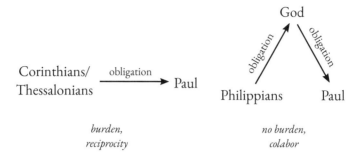

Figure 4.2: Corinthian/Thessalonian Giving vs. Philippian Giving

sense—they render it to God. Just as Old Testament Israel sacrificed to God by giving to his priests, the New Testament church often sacrifices to God by giving to his ministers.

Conclusion

The dorean principle resolves this problem of "burden" nicely, contrasting reciprocity with colabor. If the Corinthians or Thessalonians exchange material support for the gospel, they implicitly acknowledge themselves indebted to the gospel proclaimer, "burdened." However, if Paul anticipates—or even expects—their colabor, he does not burden them because he suggests no direct obligation to himself. Instead, they find themselves directly obligated to Christ, one whose burden is light (Matt. 11:30).

This conclusion aligns with Paul's consistent use of this term in the active voice. He is concerned that *he* will burden *them*, not that they may be burdened in general. Those who offer support as colabor may give out of their obligation to God, but the apostle lays no burden on anyone, including the Philippians.

5

The Prerogative of Servanthood

Freedom vs. Duty

During my senior year in high school, my parents went away on a week-long trip. They hired a babysitter (we'll call her Ann) for my 8-year-old sister, but truth be told, my sophomore brother and I probably needed one as well. Ann came highly recommended, so my parents paid her generously and left her well-supplied with additional cash in case of emergencies.

However, Ann was far from responsible. She took all the extra money and purchased junk food, primarily jelly beans. Yes, jelly beans. You can imagine how many jelly beans a decent supply of emergency cash would buy. Beyond her initial transgression, she gave my brother and me permission to go out at intervals and hours beyond the guidelines my parents had set. While I was not always the best-behaved teenager, my nefarious use of this freedom only extended to joining some study groups I wouldn't otherwise have joined. If you want to know how my brother took advantage of the opportunity, you'll have to ask him.

When my parents returned, they were less than thrilled. Ann did not receive additional employment in the Owens household.

Did Ann have a right to do as she did? In a sense, yes. When my parents hired her, they essentially gave her permission to perform all the tasks of a caretaker in their absence. This includes spending money allotted for food or deciding how to keep the kids in line. That being said, my parents expected Ann to use this authority in line with *their* priorities rather than with her own.

In his epistles, Paul frequently speaks of his right to financial support. However, he speaks of this right in the context of his *servant-hood*. Just as parents grant a babysitter jurisdiction over a home to uphold their priorities, a servant wields a delegated authority in order to accomplish his master's priorities.

In Chapter 3, we examined the triangle of obligation in 1 Corinthians 9:7–14, skipping v. 12. In this chapter, I would like us to return to that verse in order to explore how servanthood shapes Paul's use of his authority, his apostolic prerogative. Afterward, we will continue our consideration of servanthood in 1 Corinthians 9:15–22, picking up where we left off.

The Right of Servanthood

Paul's most intense defense of his refusal to accept payment appears in 1 Corinthians 9. He presents his decision in the context of Christian liberty (1 Cor. 9:19) and his right to receive support.

> If others share this rightful claim on you, do not we even more? Nevertheless, we have not made use of this right, but we endure anything rather than put an obstacle in the way of the gospel of Christ. (1 Cor. 9:12)

This has led some interpreters to decide that Paul arbitrates his policy as a matter of personal choice. In other words, it appears as though he has a permissive license to accept payment in return for his preaching but for noble reasons rejects it. At least two considerations should lead us to dismiss this claim.

First, to say that Paul goes beyond what is required of him is to identify a good course and a better course, and to declare that both are sufficiently pleasing to God. This idea is known as *supererogation* and runs contrary to the teaching of the Bible. The Lord does not require a minimum bar but perfection (Matt. 5:48). While God may require different things of different people given their strengths and circumstances, each person must serve the Lord as best he is able. Moreover, Jesus summarily dismisses this notion of supererogation when he points out that no servant of God will be able to say he has done more than was required.

> So you also, when you have done all that you were commanded, say, 'We are unworthy servants; we have only done what was our duty.' (Luke 17:10)

If one cannot do more than their duty, we can rule out the idea that it would be acceptable for Paul to accept payment but better for him to reject it.

Second, the surrounding context indicates that Paul could still be held guilty for improperly taking support, even if he has a "right" to that support. Paul's mention of his financial policy in 1 Corinthians 9 does not stand on its own but serves as an illustration to correct the Corinthians' disposition toward idolatry, addressed more directly in chapters 8 and 10. In these chapters, the apostle acknowledges the Corinthians' "right" (1 Cor. 8:9) to food but instructs them to flee idolatry (1 Cor. 10:4) and cease to eat food sacrificed to idols. To paraphrase, he describes their actions as "lawful but not helpful" (1 Cor. 10:23), meaning that though they have a right to eat, they abuse that right by eating food sacrificed to idols, committing idolatry. Notice that elsewhere, Paul uses this same distinction between "lawful" and "helpful" to describe sexual immorality (1 Cor. 6:12–15)—Christians have a right to use their bodies for sex, but they abuse that right if they sleep with a prostitute.

In other words, when Paul uses the word "right," he does not indicate a permissive license or legal *carte blanche* that justifies any course of action. Rather, he denotes an *authority of servanthood* that grants the actor freedom to serve the Lord as the Lord requires. In other words, he speaks of a stewardship. A steward has authority over an estate to do as he determines, but he incurs moral guilt when he abuses this authority to act contrary to the will of the owner. Remember Ann the babysitter? She had the right to spend the emergency fund as she chose but was still guilty when she chose poorly.

To further illustrate, Adam had stewardship over the whole garden of Eden, including the tree of the knowledge of good and evil, but this authority did not permit him to eat of that tree without penalty (Gen. 2:15–17). Likewise, the Corinthians have stewardship over their own bodies to eat food but would abuse that stewardship by eating food offered to demons (1 Cor. 10:20–21). As a servant of God, Paul has stewardship over his converts to receive money from them but would abuse that stewardship by receiving payment for a gospel that is not his to sell.

With these considerations in mind, we must conclude that Paul's financial policy does not merely represent his own preferences, a personal quirk, but an absolute ethical code. His pattern establishes a prescription that binds all who minister in the name of Christ.

The Boast of Servanthood

In 1 Corinthians 9:15–19, Paul lists several reasons for rejecting Corinthian funds, beginning with his desire to maintain grounds for boasting.

> But I have made no use of any of these rights, nor am I writing these things to secure any such provision. For I would rather die than have anyone deprive me of my ground for boasting. (1 Cor. 9:15)

Of course, boasting in himself would contradict the message of Paul's epistle (1 Cor. 1:29; 3:21; 4:7). As he writes, "Let the one who boasts, boast in the Lord" (1 Cor. 1:31; cf. 15:31). If Paul's boasting rests in the Lord independent of himself, then it resides there unthreatened, secure in an unchanging God. Yet, all the same, he declares that an acceptance of money would jeopardize his boasting, a fact he confirms in 2 Corinthians 11:7–10. In this same context he repeats the aphorism to "boast in the Lord," explaining that he boasts in the ministry God has assigned to him (2 Cor. 10:13–17). In other words, his boast in the Lord is not independent of himself; it has some relation to his ministry. Thus, an alteration to his fundraising practices potentially alters his boast.

If Paul receives direct payment from the Corinthians in exchange for his ministry, he receives honor over God as the source of the gospel. This would make his own work his grounds for boasting rather than the Lord's work. If instead he rejects payment in return for the gospel, the apostle acknowledges that its source lies outside of himself. Reciprocity compromises Paul's earnest boast in the Lord by placing his boast in himself.

The Obligation of Servanthood

Paul additionally explains that he does not accept funding from the Corinthians because he is bound to minister to them.

> For if I preach the gospel, that gives me no ground for boasting. For necessity is laid upon me. Woe to me if I do not preach the gospel! (1 Cor. 9:16)

Paul is a steward of the mysteries of God and servant of Christ (1 Cor. 4:1). Because of his status as a servant-steward, he receives no special accolades for preaching the gospel. However, if he operates as an independent agent, doing his own will rather than the will of God, it would make sense that he receives a reward, direct payment from others.

In the same way, it is improper for a royal soldier to accept money from the citizens he protects (cf. 1 Cor. 9:7). His commission from the king delegitimizes all other compensatory transactions. If he demands funding from the common man, as though their taxes are owed to him rather than the throne, he may be found guilty of extortion. Even if he only accepts voluntary offerings as support, he engages in bribery. Ultimately, the soldier who accepts any form of direct payment from the citizens ceases to operate on behalf of the king as one who is obligated but begins acting in his own interests as one who does his work freely. Similarly, if Paul were to accept money from the Corinthians as direct (i.e., unmediated) payment for his ministry there, he would invalidate his status as a servant of Christ.

As one commissioned by God, Paul cannot rightly accept third-party compensation in direct exchange for his ministry (cf. 2 Cor. 2:17). Such reciprocity denotes an insincere stewardship. However, through the dorean principle, he may accept funds that are not designed to displace his true employer. Colabor in no way invalidates Paul's status as a servant. Rather, we should *anticipate* that servants of the same master assist each other, pooling their resources as would be profitable in service of their mutual lord.

The Reward of Servanthood

In the next two verses, Paul explains that he conducts his ministry as he does in order to receive a reward.

> For if I do this of my own will, I have a reward, but if not of my own will, I am still entrusted with a stewardship. What then is my reward? That in my preaching I may present the gospel free of charge, so as not to make full use of my right in the gospel. (1 Cor. 9:17–18)

Surprisingly, Paul's activity and reward are identical: to preach the gospel free of charge. The idea is not that the apostle, by refusing money, accrues merit with which he will receive a reward. Instead, by refusing money he enjoys the reward itself—the stewardship he executes, Christ working through him. Given the preceding context of boasting (1 Cor. 9:15–16), we should not distinguish Paul's boasting from his reward. In the words of one commentator, they "refer to the same reality."[1] In either the framework of *boasting* or that of *reward*, Paul stands to gain from preaching free of charge because then Christ may be seen working through him.

In contrast, if Paul were to receive payment, his reward would be the payment itself. He would operate as a voluntary laborer setting his own fees, so he would no longer function as a servant bound by his master (cf. John 7:18). Thus, accepting financial reward would forfeit the greater reward: godly stewardship. This recalls the teaching of Christ in the Sermon on the Mount.

---

[1] Fee, *The First Epistle to the Corinthians*, 421.

> Thus, when you give to the needy, sound no trumpet
> before you, as the hypocrites do in the synagogues and
> in the streets, that they may be praised by others. Truly,
> I say to you, they have received their reward. … And
> when you fast, do not look gloomy like the hypocrites,
> for they disfigure their faces that their fasting may be
> seen by others. Truly, I say to you, they have received
> their reward. (Matt. 6:2, 16)

Using this construct, we may paraphrase Paul: "When you minister, do not be like the hypocrites, who do so for payment. Truly, I say to you, they have received their reward." Perhaps the term "hypocrite" seems too charged for the context of 1 Corinthians 9, but is not this precisely what he communicates? The one who receives reciprocity does not operate as a sincere servant of Christ but as a free agent after his own reward. On the other hand, the one who receives colabor enjoys financial benefits within the auspices of stewardship, a greater reward than mere money.

The Scope of Servanthood

In perhaps the most defining passage in 1 Corinthians 9, Paul proclaims that he has "become all things to all people."

> For though I am free from all, I have made myself a
> servant to all, that I might win more of them. To the
> Jews I became as a Jew, in order to win Jews. To those
> under the law I became as one under the law (though
> not being myself under the law) that I might win those
> under the law. To those outside the law I became as one
> outside the law (not being outside the law of God but
> under the law of Christ) that I might win those outside
> the law. To the weak I became weak, that I might win
> the weak. I have become all things to all people, that by
> all means I might save some. (1 Cor. 9:19–22)

Paul does not speak of making the gospel more attractive. He has already admitted that the gospel itself is a stumbling block, unappealing to the world (1 Cor. 1:23), and that he has eschewed typical means of attraction and persuasion (1 Cor. 2:1–5).

Furthermore, rather than stirring up goodwill through offering the gospel free of charge, we learn in 2 Corinthians that Paul only stirred up tension as those with more financially glorious ministries turned the people away to different teaching (2 Cor. 11:7). Between a free gospel and one offered at a price, the Corinthians, who so valued wealth and status in their leaders, found the latter more enticing!

While many have read 1 Corinthians 9 to speak of Paul's contextualizing of the gospel, something more specific is at play: Each of these phrases of accommodation represents some act of humility.[2] Though already a Jew, the apostle voluntarily became a Jew under the judgment of the law by receiving thirty-nine lashes (2 Cor. 11:24). He became as one without the law, renouncing all of his own merit based on law-keeping (Gal. 4:12). He became weak by enduring the hardships and humiliations of ministry (2 Cor. 12:9). These "accommodations" impress no one, yet are necessary for the gospel to go forward.

The key to all of this may be found in v. 19. Paul does not *imitate* all but rather humbles himself in order to *serve* all. As a servant of Christ, Paul must also be a servant to those to whom he is sent (2 Cor. 4:5; cf. 1:24). He does not generally act like a Jew for Jews, or a Gentile for Gentiles, or a weak person for the weak, but he is a servant to all in every circumstance by humbling himself so that the truth of the gospel may be properly acknowledged. We should not be misguided by the apostle's clever rhetorical device, imagining that he would become popular for the popular, strong for the strong, or rich for the rich.

The same applies to Paul's rejection of money. First-century Corinth bustled with economic prosperity, and certainly some of the wealthy filled the ranks in the church (cf. 1 Cor. 4:8), so Paul does not reject financial support out of a desire to blend in. He does not make himself attractive to the people of Corinth; as we have seen, accepting their money would have made him more attractive. Rather,

---

[2] See David E. Garland's commentary for further demonstrations that each of these phrases represents an act of humility. Garland, *1 Corinthians*, 427–437.

he humbles himself so that he might fulfill the role of a servant.

Here, sincerity and rejection of reciprocity go hand-in-hand. If Paul were to accept payment from the Corinthians, he would not be their servant but a service provider and they his clients. Whether or not he requests money, his ministry would be understood to impose an obligation that requires a settling of accounts. However, the apostle may freely accept material support from colaborers without compromising his position.

Conclusion

The duty of servanthood demands the dorean principle. As a servant, Paul must reject ministerial reciprocity, and he must accept ministerial colabor. In the next chapter, we will look at Paul's motivations through an additional lens: his sincerity.

6

The Sincerity of Ministry

Pragmatism vs. Principle

I did not have a lasting career in the world of theater, but I did enjoy the time I spent in it. At one point, I had the privilege of being cast in a community production of *The Fantasticks*.

If you are unfamiliar with the musical, the first act models the plot of *Romeo and Juliet* but ends more comically than the Shakespearean tragedy. Two young lovers pursue each other while their feuding families attempt to keep them apart. Through their perseverance, they happily marry. However, the couple struggles to keep their relationship together in the second act when they discover the family conflict was all a ruse. Their fathers only pretended to fight in order to matchmake the rebellious youths, who they were certain would do exactly what they told them not to do and fall in love with exactly whom they told them not to fall in love with.

The word "pragmatic" best describes the two fathers in *The Fantasticks*. While other parents might be driven by principles such as honesty or liberty, these fathers were dead set on accomplishing the match through whatever means they had available to them. This divide between pragmatism and principle applies to our consideration of Paul's ministry.

Most people would not regard the apostle Paul as a devious manipulator. Regardless, many label his refusal of funds as an act of pragmatism—an otherwise morally neutral course of action taken in order to advance the gospel with minimal impediment. Sometimes Paul refuses funds in order to promote an industrious work ethic, sometimes he refuses funds in order to satisfy the expectations of his audience, sometimes he refuses funds in order to accommodate the impoverished, sometimes he refuses funds in order to avoid conflicts of interest, and so on.

In the course of this book, I have taken a different approach, rejecting the notion that Paul primarily acts out of various pragmatic motivations. Rather, I have identified the apostle as a principled actor following a singular moral code set by Christ. Yet, this code itself is not without its own underlying motivation. Paul does not promote obedience to an arbitrary rule but instead highlights the virtue that undergirds the dorean principle and its rejection of reciprocity. While he indeed speaks of gospel reach and other motivations, he primarily emphasizes the importance of *sincerity*. He states the matter most directly in his second epistle to the Corinthians.

> For we are not, like so many, peddlers of God's word,
> but as men of sincerity, as commissioned by God, in the
> sight of God we speak in Christ. (2 Cor. 2:17)

Paul identifies the peddling of God's word—i.e., receiving in exchange for ministry—as the opposite of sincerity. While the apostle occasionally mentions other factors that motivate his policy, this goal sits at the core of his intentions.

In this chapter, we will explore a handful of Paul's stated motivations, examining how they align with the virtue of sincerity. These motivations certainly voice Paul's concern for the spread of the gospel, but they ultimately clear his name from charges of pragmatism. More importantly, they reveal sincerity's discord with reciprocity as well its harmony with colabor.

Sincere Ministry

In the previous chapter, we saw that Paul waives his right to support in order to maintain his status as a servant. It naturally follows that he

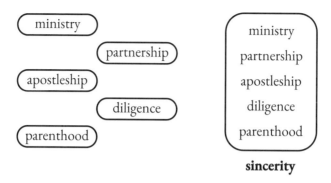

Figure 6.1: Disparate Motivations vs. Unified Motivation

must abide by the dorean principle in order to serve *sincerely*. While he primarily speaks of his service to the Lord in 1 Corinthians 9, he also speaks of his service to others (1 Cor. 9:19). This continues in 2 Corinthians 11, where the apostle claims that he preaches free of charge in order to "exalt" others.

> Or did I commit a sin in humbling myself so that you might be exalted, because I preached God's gospel to you free of charge? (2 Cor. 11:7)

While Paul's humility is physical, the Corinthians' exaltation is spiritual. That is, the apostle exalts the Corinthians through their salvation; they have been raised up and seated in the heavenly places (Eph. 2:6). The preceding context redefines this exaltation in terms of betrothal to Christ (2 Cor. 11:2). If his goal is the salvation of the Corinthians, then Paul rejects funds in order that he can *rightly* or *effectively* preach the gospel.

On either of these counts, Paul's free preaching extends from his sincerity. If it is necessary to preach freely in order to preach rightly, he will do so because he ministers sincerely, without ulterior motive. If it is necessary to preach freely in order to preach effectively, he will do so because he sincerely desires Corinthian exaltation. Paul argues that his rejection of payment is an expression of love for the Corinthians

(2 Cor. 11:11; cf. Gal. 4:16). Anything else would be insincere (cf. 2 Cor. 2:17), not truly a pursuit of love.

Sincere Apostleship

As Paul's ministry is in his apostleship, it stands to reason that sincere ministry demands sincere apostleship. Thus, when false apostles began leading people astray in Corinth, Paul appeals to his fidelity to the dorean principle in order to demonstrate the truth of his apostleship. As his opponents have not lived up to the same standard, this same principle demonstrates their false apostleship. Speaking of his rejection of funds, Paul writes,

> And what I am doing I will continue to do, in order to undermine the claim of those who would like to claim that in their boasted mission they work on the same terms as we do. (2 Cor. 11:12)

Paul chooses rejection of payment as a marker of delineation between himself and others who claim to have a similar apostolic ministry—and his choice of this particular distinctive is not arbitrary. If his actions are to cut off opportunity from his opponents to claim apostolicity, what he does must actually mark his ministry as true, not merely different.

As the Greek word *apostolos* indicates, an apostle is *sent*, and this commission entails a certain behavior toward those to whom he is sent. He must share his message indiscriminately and without return from the recipients of his message, not adopting the commercial practices of one who has ulterior motives. This practice and attitude distinguish Paul from his opponents in 2 Corinthians. With this contrast in mind, he pens the following words: "For we are not, like so many, peddlers of God's word," (2 Cor. 2:17a).

Sincere Parenthood

Later in 2 Corinthians, Paul speaks of his spiritual fatherhood.

> Here for the third time I am ready to come to you. And
> I will not be a burden, for I seek not what is yours but
> you. For children are not obligated to save up for their
> parents, but parents for their children. (2 Cor. 12:14; cf.
> 1 Thess. 2:5–7, 9–12).

This language of paternity highlights Paul's role in the conversion of the Corinthians. Thus, he says that he became a father to the Corinthians in the gospel (1 Cor. 4:15). Similarly, he birthed his Galatian children through the formation of Christ within them (Gal. 4:19), and he became Onesimus's father upon Onesimus's conversion (Philem. 10–11).

This metaphor of paternity provides an illustration of why it would be particularly inappropriate for Paul to engage in ministerial reciprocity with his church plants. While others might receive payment from their converts, Paul declines because this would be akin to a father burdening his child. He rejects their money out of love (2 Cor. 11:11). He repeats this paternal ethic to the Thessalonians, contrasting greed and parenthood.

As their spiritual father, Paul must act sincerely as a parent rather than with a "pretext for greed."

> For we never came with words of flattery, as you know,
> nor with a pretext for greed—God is witness. Nor did
> we seek glory from people, whether from you or from
> others, though we could have made demands as apostles
> of Christ. But we were gentle among you, like a nursing
> mother taking care of her own children. (1 Thess. 2:5–7)

Yet in a sense, Paul does demand a form of repayment for his fatherly love: "In return (I speak as to children) widen your hearts also." (2 Cor. 6:13). While the apostle does not burden his children by accepting payment for his ministry, he demands the repayment of love and honor. In context, they are to do this by receiving his appeal to be reconciled to God (2 Cor. 5:20). In other words, sincere parenthood warrants sincere childlike deference. If Paul desires to secure the cooperation of his converts, he must reject their payment as a loving father.

Sincere Diligence

In Thessalonica, Paul refuses funds in order to set an example of hard work.

> For you yourselves know how you ought to imitate us, because we were not idle when we were with you, nor did we eat anyone's bread without paying for it, but with toil and labor we worked night and day, that we might not be a burden to any of you. It was not because we do not have that right, but to give you in ourselves an example to imitate. (2 Thess. 3:7–9)

Some have taken these comments to mean that though Paul has no obligation to engage in manual labor, he does so in order to offer a lesson on work ethic. However, if preaching and teaching are labors worthy of reward (cf. 1 Tim. 5:17), why are they not sufficient examples for the Thessalonians? Since Paul could undoubtedly work diligently as an apostle while refraining from physical labor, there must be some illegitimacy in accepting payment for his ministry.

Indeed, there is. The preceding epistle to the Thessalonians clarifies the matter, contrasting "a pretext for greed" (1 Thess. 2:5) with Paul's statement that "we worked night and day" (1 Thess. 2:9; cf. 2 Thess. 3:8). To receive payment from converts would be greedy and therefore lazy, contrary to the diligence required of God's servants. Sincere diligence demands forgoing ministerial reciprocity.

Paul's ethic appears again as an example in his parting message to Ephesus.

> I coveted no one's silver or gold or apparel. You yourselves know that these hands ministered to my necessities and to those who were with me. In all things I have shown you that by working hard in this way we must help the weak and remember the words of the Lord Jesus, how he himself said, 'It is more blessed to give than to receive.' (Acts 20:33–35)

The apostle pits manual labor (ministering to his own needs) against covetousness. In other words, sincere diligence in the work of ministry requires the rejection of unmediated payment. He identifies anything else as greed. Furthermore, he must help the weak by ministering freely; to minister for pay would not be sufficient.

By rejecting support in contexts where it would constitute direct payment, Paul sets an example of hard work. However, this example is not grounded in arbitrary illustrative toil but in the sincere diligence required by the dorean principle.

Sincere Partnership

Finally, returning to 1 Corinthians 9, Paul selectively refuses financial support so that he may be a partner in the work of the gospel. He gives priority to this motivation when he chooses to summarize his concerns with the following words.

> I do all things for the sake of the gospel, so that I may become a fellow partaker of it. (1 Cor. 9:23, NASB)

The Greek word for "fellow partaker" here derives from *koinonia*, the word used to refer to partnership in Philippians. In this verse, many translations speak of the gospel and sharing in "its blessings." However, this elaboration shifts the focus from the proclamation of the gospel to the rewards of the gospel and potentially misses the point of Paul's argument. Having stated his sincere desire for the salvation of others, he does not suddenly reveal that he is primarily concerned for his own salvation or that he hopes to benefit as his converts do. Here and in the following context, he speaks of sharing in the gospel as a minister of it. Describing himself as an athlete striving for a reward in vv. 24–27, Paul does not imagine himself meriting the gift of salvation, but winning the special prize due to faithful ministers (cf. 1 Cor. 3:14).

In 1 Corinthians 9:23, it is best to see Paul as sharing in *the work of the gospel*. The preceding context confirms this. The apostle has explained that causing another to stumble is to oppose the gospel, but here he offers the alternative: to lead one to salvation is to be its partner. Furthermore, this use of the word "gospel" without an attendant verb frequently indicates the *proclamation* of the gospel

(Rom. 1:1; 1 Cor. 9:14; 2 Cor. 2:12; 10:14; Gal. 2:7; Phil. 2:22; 4:15).[1] In the words of one pair of commentators, "Paul's overriding allegiance is as *a partner of the gospel*."[2]

On many occasions, Paul rejects financial support so that he might sincerely partner in the work of ministry. Other times, his reception of funds does not compromise that goal. On those occasions, those who support him are his partners (cf. Phil. 4:15). Evidencing the notion of colabor, this passage reveals Paul's motivation of sincerity. Rather than only putting on the appearance of a fellow worker, he selectively accepts support so he might engage in sincere partnership.

Conclusion

Notions of earnestness and veracity resound behind all of Paul's explicit motivations for rejecting payment. The apostle operates as a sincere servant, a sincere apostle, a sincere father, and a sincere partner. To wholeheartedly do what he has been called to do and genuinely be what he has been called to be, he must reject ministerial reciprocity.

Sincerity propels the dorean principle. That is, *dorean ministry is sincere ministry*. In the next chapter, we will see that the Bible identifies all non-dorean ministry as insincere, the work of false teachers.

---

[1] See Hooker, "A Partner in the Gospel," 87; Schütz, *Paul and the Anatomy of Apostolic Authority*, 53.

[2] Orr and Walther, *I Corinthians*, 243.

7

The Greed of Wolves

Feature vs. Essence

About a year ago, I moved into a new home with a small tree in the backyard. I was thinking about removing the tree until winter came around and one of my kids found something interesting on it. It was an orange, and a tasty one at that! I decided not to uproot the tree but keep it. As Jesus said, a good tree bears good fruit.

However, unlike me and my orange tree, Christ's concern did not revolve around identifying literal dead plants. Specifically, he wanted to equip his disciples to recognize and reject false teachers.

> Beware of false prophets, who come to you in sheep's clothing but inwardly are ravenous wolves. You will recognize them by their fruits. Are grapes gathered from thornbushes, or figs from thistles? So, every healthy tree bears good fruit, but the diseased tree bears bad fruit. A healthy tree cannot bear bad fruit, nor can a diseased tree bear good fruit. Every tree that does not bear good fruit is cut down and thrown into the fire. Thus you will recognize them by their fruits. (Matt. 7:15–20)

A bad orange tree might produce bad oranges or even no oranges at all, but what does a false teacher produce? Of course, false teaching is the characteristic staple of a false teacher, but Jesus reveals some-

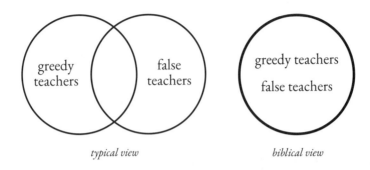

Figure 7.1: The Relationship Between Greed and False Teaching

thing more in this passage. He describes these malefactors as ravenous wolves, implying an underlying motivation of greed.

One may play down greed as merely a peripheral feature of false teachers, but the recurring drumbeat of the New Testament places it at the heart of all false teaching. We could imagine a false teacher who lives a life of poverty, but the issue does not revolve around money so much as it does the pursuit of personal benefit. Indeed, if one does not serve Christ, he has in mind his own gain (cf. Matt. 6:24). In other words, the *falseness* of a false teacher does not merely hinge on erroneous doctrine, but on the teacher himself. Dentures are regarded as false teeth though they may bite and chew like real teeth. Likewise, one who seeks his own gain in ministry is a false teacher though he may promote a similar authentic doctrine.

As we saw in the previous chapter, Paul's rejection of ministerial reciprocity extends from his sincerity—i.e., his lack of ulterior motive. Conversely, all who minister with an eye toward material payment possess an ulterior motive, unveiling themselves as less than sincere, as false teachers. This observation elevates the dorean principle beyond a nice-to-have idea. If the New Testament anticipates that we should be able to distinguish false teachers from true teachers by their disposition toward reciprocity, then the dorean principle is an essential component of God-honoring ministry.

In this chapter, I would like to walk through several examples of false teachers in the New Testament. In each one, we will see greed tied tightly to their identity, further establishing that true ministry needs to be marked with the sincerity of the dorean principle.

The Scribes and Pharisees

Notably, the scribes and Pharisees fall directly into this category of false teachers. While some of their expansive rules and allowances are at odds with a proper understanding of God's law, the New Testament regards the Pharisees as the contemporary sect of Judaism with the highest doctrinal fidelity. In other words, they taught with more accuracy than any other group of their day (cf. Acts 23:6; 26:5; Phil. 3:5). Nevertheless, Jesus condemns them as false teachers, largely on account of their greed.

> Beware of the scribes, who like to walk round in long robes, and love greetings in the marketplaces and the best seats in the synagogues and the places of honor at feasts, who devour widows' houses and for a pretense make long prayers. They will receive the greater condemnation. (Luke 20:46–47; cf. Matt. 23:15, 25).

Each of these criticisms focuses on covetousness rather than on doctrinal error. The scribes desire honor in the form of recognition and material gain. Jesus presents this greed not merely as an arbitrary vice that attends the actions of the scribes, but as something central that drives their evil deeds.

Notice also the pattern by which Jesus exposes a heart of covetousness in this passage. It is not long robes or greetings that are wrong but the love of prestige. Long prayers are not problematic, but pretense is abhorrent. However, Jesus interrupts this pattern when he speaks of widows' houses. Here, the matter goes beyond the intentions of the heart. Christ describes the action itself in such a way that it could not accord with pure motives. To devour another's property is to maliciously harm them. At this point, when material wealth is in view, the heart issue present in each of the other criticisms becomes most directly manifest.

This identity between insincerity and the pursuit of wealth echoes in John 10, where Jesus alludes to the Pharisees of the previous chapter, describing them as hired hands.

> He who is a hired hand and not a shepherd, who does not own the sheep, sees the wolf coming and leaves the sheep and flees, and the wolf snatches them and scatters them. He flees because he is a hired hand and cares nothing for the sheep. (John 10:12–13)

Jesus offers no accusation of excess, as though ministers should strive for some ethic of moderation that the hired hand has violated by demanding more than reasonable compensation. The ulterior motive of gain—in any quantity—sufficiently incriminates the hired hand, differentiating him from the shepherd. Even here in the pages of the gospels, the New Testament prepares us to identify greed—the pursuit of ministry for the sake of earthly recompense—as the identifying marker of false teachers.

Simon the Magician

The narrative of Simon the magician in Acts stands out among encounters between money and ministry.

> Now when Simon saw that the Spirit was given through the laying on of the apostles' hands, he offered them money, saying, "Give me this power also, so that anyone on whom I lay my hands may receive the Holy Spirit." But Peter said to him, "May your silver perish with you, because you thought you could obtain the gift of God with money! You have neither part nor lot in this matter, for your heart is not right before God. (Acts 8:18–21)

Do not mistake the ethical transgression for a misunderstanding about the mechanics of impartation. Explicitly, Peter rebukes Simon because he thought the gift of God *could* be obtained by money. Implicitly, the apostle rebukes the magician because he thought the gift of God *ought* to be given for money. Simon treats Peter as a minister for profit and sets himself up to potentially become one as well, doling out this power to others who have the coin to spare.

By virtue of its narrative form, this passage centers around the particulars of one individual, Simon. However, the prominence of this event in the fledgling church signifies the divine delivery of a generalized principle. It is not merely it *impossible* to facilitate the distribution of the gift of the Holy Spirit by means of financial exchange; it is *dishonorable* to make any such attempt. Broadly speaking, any ministry—miraculous or non-miraculous—constitutes an attempt to impart the blessing of the Holy Spirit. In this light, the passage condemns all ministerial reciprocity. In the words of D. A. Carson, "Those who charge for spiritual ministry are dabbling in simony."[1]

The Balaamites

Both Peter and Jude compare false teachers at large to Balaam, the prophet willing to prophesy ill for a price.[2] After two explicit mentions of greed (2 Pet. 2:3, 14), Peter speaks broadly of the false teachers who will arise:

> Forsaking the right way, they have gone astray. They have followed the way of Balaam, the son of Beor, who loved gain from wrongdoing, … (2 Pet. 2:15)

Jude offers a similar description of false teachers:

> Woe to them! For they walked in the way of Cain and abandoned themselves for the sake of gain to Balaam's error and perished in Korah's rebellion. (Jude 11)

By evoking the name of Balaam, Peter and Jude describe false teachers as primarily motivated by greed.

Additionally, both Peter and Jude employ the descriptor "sensuality" to characterize false teachers' desire for worldly pleasures (2 Pet.

---

[1] Carson, *When Jesus Confronts the World*, 141.

[2] Perhaps it is not evident why Balaam would be associated with greed, but this was a common assertion in contemporary Jewish literature, derived from Numbers 24:13. See Ginzberg, *The Legends of the Jews*, 3.360.

2:2; Jude 4). While this likely refers to the licentious teachings of the false teachers, the connection to material greed should not be missed. Peter offers "greed" as an immediate expansion on the term "sensuality" (2 Pet. 2:2–3). Jude associates Balaamistic greed with animalistic impulses (Jude 10–11). Though "sensuality" primarily connotes sexual implications, it more broadly refers to all the desires of the flesh. Note that even the tenth commandment (thou shalt not covet) unites the notions of greed and lust. Peter's introduction of Balaam hints at this link, spelling his father's name in Greek as "Bosor" rather than "Beor." That is, Peter identifies Balaam as a son of the flesh, transliterating the Hebrew word for "flesh" rather than the actual name of Balaam's father.[3]

Jude further exposes this connection between greed and fleshly desire in his mention of shepherds feeding themselves (Jude 12), an allusion to Ezekiel 34:1–10 and the shepherds of Israel who preyed on the sheep. Similarly, Paul speaks of false teachers as being motivated by their appetites (Rom. 16:18) and having their bellies as their gods (Phil. 3:19), most likely referring to their desire for compensation.

2 Peter and Jude place greed at the heart of false teaching. The motivation of wealth stands at odds with the path of a true teacher.

The Money Lovers

Whether they represent a single party or not, Paul depicts the false teachers of the pastoral epistles as lovers of money. Though their origin and many of their beliefs are uncertain, "What is clear from Paul's words in the Pastoral Epistles is the motivation of false teachers. It is 'greed.'"[4]

In 1 Timothy 6:3–10, the apostle warns against false teachers, listing their various qualities. Finally, he settles on the assertion that false teachers consider godliness to be a means of gain (1 Tim. 6:5).

---

[3]See Luther, *Commentary on Peter and Jude*, 272; Bauckham, *Jude, 2 Peter*, 267–268.

[4]Verbrugge and Krell, *Paul and Money*, 247.

> If anyone teaches a different doctrine and does not agree
> with the sound words of our Lord Jesus Christ and the
> teaching that accords with godliness, he is puffed up with
> conceit and understands nothing. He has an unhealthy
> craving for controversy and for quarrels about words,
> which produce envy, dissension, slander, evil suspicions,
> and constant friction among people who are depraved in
> mind and deprived of the truth, imagining that godliness
> is a means of gain. (1 Tim. 6:3–5)

Notably, Paul phrases his rebuke to address *all* false teachers,
speaking of *any* who teach a different doctrine. He may have in mind
particular false teachers, but that does not limit the scope of his application, which is put forward as a general principle. The apostle's
profile of a false teacher includes the invariable element of greed, that
fundamental component that compromises sincere ministry.

Paul addresses lovers of money in 2 Timothy 3:2, again describing
them as having a superficial godliness (2 Tim. 3:5). Additionally, he
compares them to Jannes and Jambres.

> Just as Jannes and Jambres opposed Moses, so these men
> also oppose the truth, men corrupted in mind and dis-
> qualified regarding the faith. (2 Tim. 3:8)

These two are not mentioned in the Old Testament, but Jewish
tradition records them as magicians in the employ of Pharaoh, appren-
tices of the prophet Balaam.[5] Not only does service to Pharaoh indicate the pursuit of riches (cf. Heb. 11:25), but as we have already seen,
the apostles used Balaam's name synonymously with greed-driven
prophecy. This issue of false teachers and the love of money is undoubtedly the same warning that was issued in the previous epistle
to Timothy. Once again, Paul highlights the love of money as the
standard trait of false teachers.

Likewise, in his epistle to Titus, Paul contrasts true teaching with
false teaching. In particular, he warns against the "circumcision party."

---

[5] See Ginzberg, *The Legends of the Jews*, 2.335.

> They must be silenced, since they are upsetting whole
> families by teaching for shameful gain what they ought
> not to teach. (Titus 1:11)

The doctrines of the "circumcision party" are not altogether certain, but the New Testament presents this faction as a prototypical band of false teachers (cf. Gal. 2:12; Acts 11:2). This is significant. By withholding details of their beliefs while painting a robust picture of their motivations, Scripture offers a generalized teaching in a particularized context. The core accusations applied to this sect are intended to apply broadly to false teachers of any sect. This passage does not merely offer greed as a potential trait of false teachers but as something that universally characterizes them. All false teachers are motivated by greed, and all teachers motivated by greed are false.

Requirements for Elders

In the New Testament, established requirements for elders function as guards against false teachers assuming the office. It is significant, therefore, that these listings of qualifications invariably prohibit greed. Each passage regards greed not merely as an unbecoming attribute of a true teacher but as a mark of a false teacher.

This connection appears most strikingly in Titus, where the description of a true teacher (Titus 1:5–9) is placed in immediate contrast with the description of a false teacher (Titus 1:10–16). In particular, an elder is not to be greedy for "shameful gain" (Titus 1:7) because there are many false teachers who teach for the sake of "shameful gain" (Titus 1:11).

1 Timothy 3:3 plainly forbids an elder not to be a "lover of money." Later in the same epistle, Paul describes the "love of money" as the hallmark of false ministry, a root of all kinds of evil (1 Tim. 6:10).

1 Peter does not directly address false teaching, but its prohibition against greed stands in line with the previous passages. 1 Peter 5:2 requires that elders minister eagerly, not for shameful gain. While the contrast is not immediately apparent, these two are offered within a list of opposites. An elder is not to minister under compulsion but

willingly; he is not to be domineering but an example. In this light, eagerness stands opposed to shameful gain. Those who desire money from ministry have a competing motive. We might be quick to reduce this competing motive as problematic only when it is central to the minister, but the text does not warrant such qualifications. Any competing motivation compromises the sincerity—i.e., the eagerness—of a minister. In the words of one theologian, "At the very least, this [passage] implies that Christian leaders should not be motivated to minister by the thought of remuneration or any particular level of payment."[6]

Conclusion

Each of these passages we examined regards greed as the tell-tale characteristic of a false teacher. Wolves are not wolves apart from their ravenous appetite. So to answer our original question: What is the fruit of false teachers? Their greed. In more concrete demonstrations, it is the acceptance of reciprocity, their exchange of ministry for money.

The New Testament does not merely offer the dorean principle as a way to honor God in ministry but additionally as a way of discerning true teachers from false teachers. In a world that has lost this standard, it can hardly function as such. However, if restored, this ethic could operate as intended: as a marker of legitimate servants of the Lord. True ministers would be known for freely offering the gospel. False teachers, motivated by greed, would be recognized by their receipt of reciprocity. Lack of adherence to the dorean principle would raise a red flag, marking out wolves among sheep.

In the next chapter, we'll take a look at a particularly notable set of false teachers: the super-apostles of Corinth.

---

[6]Blomberg, *Neither Poverty nor Riches*, 230.

8

The Apostles of Corinth

Partiality vs. Equity

Are you familiar with the riddle of the green glass door? It goes something like this. I announce that there's a green glass door and that only certain things can go through the green glass door. For example, I can bring a kitten but not a cat. I can bring the moon but not the sun. I can bring a wheel but not a tire. The puzzle challenges others to figure out what kinds of things may be brought through the green glass door. They guess an object, and I tell them whether it can go through the door.

When first encountering this riddle, you might think you see some pattern. For example, the way I have set this up you might be inclined to think that the green glass door favors objects in miniature. In fact, I would agree with you that I can bring something small through the door but not something large. However, you will likely be frustrated as you test this and find that you can bring a gorilla through the door but not a chimp!

Eventually, someone in the group will discover the objects themselves don't matter at all, only their spelling. Words with double letters are permitted through, while words without double letters are not. (That's why it's called the green glass door.)

Similarly, if we only examine prominent features of the transactions he condones, Paul's financial policy may appear to operate by some arbitrary partiality. Perhaps he favors true ministers or perhaps he favors mature churches. However, beyond these red herrings lies his true objective: the dorean principle.

In Chapters 2 and 4, we used the dorean principle to resolve two apparent discrepancies in Paul's financial policy:

1. Why does Paul reject Corinthian money, yet accept Corinthian *propempo* support?

2. Why does Paul reject Corinthian and Thessalonian money, yet accept Philippian money?

We saw that Paul rejected Corinthian funds because such would constitute reciprocity, but he was willing to accept Corinthian *propempo* support because it would constitute colabor. Similarly, Paul rejected money from the Thessalonian church since it would only serve as repayment for the gospel, but he was willing to accept money from the Philippians because they contributed to Paul's resources in an act of colabor.

In this chapter, we will use the dorean principle to clear up two additional enigmas:

3. Why does Paul reject Corinthian money, yet permits other apostles to receive it?

4. Why does Paul condone the reception of Corinthian money by other apostles, yet condemn the "super-apostles" for accepting it?

Many attempts to present a unified understanding of Paul's financial policy fail because they propose solutions that can only account for a few of these apparent discrepancies. However, the dorean principle explains Paul's behavior in each instance. Though I believe I have sufficiently established the truth of the dorean principle from other texts, resolving these last two apparent discrepancies should afford us an extra level of confidence.

Paul's Disposition Toward Other Ministers

If the dorean principle dictates Paul's behavior rather than pragmatic concerns, we should see the apostle require the same behavior from his associates. Indeed, this is what we find. In fact, when he describes this policy, he frequently employs the language of "we," referring to the others who traveled with him (1 Cor. 9:11–12). For example, he explicitly names Barnabas as one who has performed manual labor to avoid taking money from the Corinthians (1 Cor. 9:6). Further, Paul remarks that he has not even been a burden through those whom he has sent, specifically mentioning Titus as one example (2 Cor. 12:17–18). And just as Paul willingly accepts *propempo* support, he commands that Timothy receive it as well (1 Cor. 16:11).

However, Paul has no objection to the Jerusalem apostles receiving freely from the Corinthians.

> Do we not have the right to eat and drink? Do we not have the right to take along a believing wife, as do the other apostles and the brothers of the Lord and Cephas? (1 Cor. 9:4–5)

Paul mentions Cephas—another name for Peter—and the brothers of the Lord—likely including James (cf. Gal. 1:19). These apostles from Jerusalem have apparently visited Corinth and received support rather than engaging in secular labor to pay their own way. Of course, Paul does not really suggest he has no right to eat or drink or have a wife. Instead, he refers to the expenses incurred by each of these things and the financial support required. In all this, Paul implicitly condones the Jerusalem apostles' reception of Corinthian support.

However, when a different group of teachers accepts money from the Corinthians, Paul condemns them harshly. These are the "super-apostles," false apostles who compete with Paul for prominence in Corinth. Toward the end of 2 Corinthians, he offers a full defense of his own rejection of funds, implicitly comparing himself to his opponents who have received funds (cf. 2 Cor. 11:7). However, even at the beginning of the epistle, he criticizes their reception of Corinthian money.

> For we are not, like so many, peddlers of God's word,
> but as men of sincerity, as commissioned by God, in the
> sight of God we speak in Christ. (2 Cor. 2:17)

Why does Paul respond so differently toward his opponents in Corinth? It might appear that he engages in partiality by labeling them "peddlers" yet turning a blind eye to the Jerusalem apostles when they accept money from the Corinthians. This accusation would stand if he condemns the super-apostles' reception of funds simply because they propagate false doctrine. However, the accusation of partiality falls apart if instead he has identified a fundamental error in their fundraising activities.

Paul's Consistency Toward the Jerusalem Apostles

After imposing a strict policy on himself and his companions, does Paul give a free pass to the apostles from Jerusalem? Once again, the dorean principle resolves this matter neatly.

In Corinth, Paul's continued refusal of money revolves around the particular sum offered on his initial visit. He regards this as payment for the gospel (cf. 1 Cor. 9:18), ministerial reciprocity. The apostle never receives money from those he is converting.[1] However, as we have already noted, Paul willingly receives money from his churches when the context does not indicate that they intend to repay him for his ministry or for their conversion.

The Jerusalem apostles arrived at an established church and would have not received the same offer that Paul received. The finances given to them must have been granted in another context, likely in the weekly contributions a church collects in order to support the proclamation of the gospel. In short, Paul condones other apostles accepting money from the Corinthians because this money would have been given as colabor. In contrast to the reciprocal offering of a grateful convert, these funds constitute the assistance of an established

---

[1]See Hock, "The Working Apostle," 127n40,133,137–1138.

Christian. The former implies a direct obligation to the minister who first shared the gospel, but the latter acknowledges an obligation mediated by God.

Paul's Consistency Toward the Super-Apostles

We see that Paul allows the Jerusalem apostles to receive money from Corinth but condemns the super-apostles when they do the same. On one hand, it seems appealing to assume Paul grants privileges to true teachers that he does not grant to false teachers. However, he calls their reception of material support burdensome, even an act of devouring (2 Cor. 11:21).[2] Labeling their financial practices abusive, he leaves no room for a true apostle to engage in the same behavior. Certainly, false apostles should not receive support due a true minister, but Paul objects to their financial practice in its own right.

In fact, Paul explicitly confirms that he holds them to the same financial standard he holds himself to.

> And what I am doing I will continue to do, in order to undermine the claim of those who would like to claim that in their boasted mission they work on the same terms as we do. (2 Cor. 11:12)

That is, Paul maintains his policy of refusing payment to show that his opponents do not live up to the same code of conduct.

In order for Paul to act consistently in this matter, he must identify the Corinthian contributions to the super-apostles as acts of ministerial reciprocity. Indeed, he does. When he responds to the objections of the super-apostles, he compares their practice of charging for the gospel to his own practice of preaching freely.

> Or did I commit a sin in humbling myself so that you might be exalted, because I preached God's gospel to you free of charge? (2 Cor. 11:7)

---

[2] For the relationship between "devouring" and the super-apostles' financial practices, see Harris, *The Second Epistle to the Corinthians*, 785.

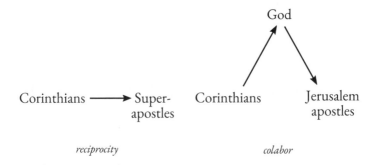

Figure 8.1: The Super-Apostles vs. The Jerusalem Apostles

In saying that he has not charged for his preaching, Paul implies that the super-apostles *have* charged for their preaching. Additionally, when he accuses them of "peddling" the gospel (2 Cor. 2:17), he condemns their activities as commercial transactions.

The super-apostles have not erred in receiving money in general but in receiving it in direct exchange for the gospel. If they instead sought to colabor with the Corinthians, Paul would not raise the same objections. The dorean principle sufficiently accounts for the disparity in the apostle's attitude toward the financial practices of his friends and toward those of his opponents.

A False Claim on Corinth

Examining the relationship between the super-apostles and Corinth, we can see why the exchange between them constitutes payment. The "ministry" of the super-apostles more closely imitates the ministry of Paul than it does that of the Jerusalem apostles. That is, the super-apostles implicitly claim his spiritual fatherhood as their own, masquerading as church planters.

Paul demonstrates this pretense most directly in 2 Corinthians 10. Arguing that the fruit of his labor serves as sufficient proof of his status, the apostle objects to his opponents' practice of self-commendation in v. 12 and v. 18. Between these bookends, he offers a comparison to his own practices.

> But we will not boast beyond limits, but will boast only with regard to the area of influence God assigned to us, to reach even to you. For we are not overextending ourselves, as though we did not reach you. For we were the first to come all the way to you with the gospel of Christ. We do not boast beyond limit in the labors of others. But our hope is that as your faith increases, our area of influence among you may be greatly enlarged, so that we may preach the gospel in lands beyond you, without boasting of work already done in another's area of influence. "Let the one who boasts, boast in the Lord." (2 Cor. 10:13–17)

When Paul claims that he does not boast beyond limits, he implies that the super-apostles *do* boast beyond limits. Terms such as "limits," "area," "overextending," "reach," etc., indicate some geographic extent, especially given that Paul pairs them with the notion of the gospel expanding beyond Corinth and Achaia (2 Cor. 10:16; 11:10). In other words, the apostle considers the church in Corinth his divinely appointed domain,[3] but his opponents consider it the fruit of their labors. Paul expresses similar concerns elsewhere, declaring that as a church planter, he does not go where Christ has been named, building on another's foundation (Rom. 15:20). On the other hand, his opponents are eager to operate as pseudo-missionaries who lay claim to another's work.

To be clear, Paul takes no issue with others building on his foundation (1 Cor. 3:6, 12–13). Rather, he objects to those who would wrongly assume the status of one who lays a foundation, hence his focus on boasting. Perhaps it is too implausible to suggest that the false apostles have explicitly labeled themselves the founders or spiritual fathers of the Corinthian church, but by his comparisons, Paul at least charges them with having implicitly done so. They overextend themselves, claiming dominion over a region they did not reach first

---

[3] See Harris, *The Second Epistle to the Corinthians*, 711–713.

(2 Cor. 10:14). They boast beyond limit in the labors of others (2 Cor. 10:15). They take credit for work already done (2 Cor. 10:16). What is that work, other than the work of church planting? If nothing else, we may say Paul's opponents encroach on the achievements of his ministry, taking evangelical credit for the spiritual prosperity of Corinth.

Placing themselves in Paul's position, the super-apostles eagerly run into the ethical transgression Paul avoided: They accept payment from their supposed converts.

A False Gospel

This brings us to a final observation: Paul never explicitly defines the false gospel of the super-apostles. He claims that his opponents come with "another Jesus," "a different spirit," and "a different gospel" (2 Cor. 11:4), but never elaborates beyond this. Perhaps Paul and the Corinthians share a mutual understanding of an unspoken issue, but the idea of leaving unaddressed some doctrinal error spreading in Corinth flies in the face of Paul's pattern and agenda. A false doctrine must be countered, and given his response to Galatia, a false gospel is so detrimental that it calls for the formal pronouncement of anathema (Gal. 1:8–9).

It seems more likely that the super-apostles represent a different Christ by falsely claiming they have been sent by Christ. Likewise, their false spirit and false gospel may be their promotion of external appearances over inner truth. Instead of exalting Christ, they exalt themselves. In this case, Paul does address their false gospel, head-on.

Rather than imagining some overt heresy that remains unspoken in the course of this epistle, we should recognize as primary those problems the apostle explicitly addresses. The false gospel of Paul's opponents is no straightforward doctrinal error but the very thing that concerns him throughout the epistle: a disposition that boasts in self instead of in the Lord.

This claim to the church in Corinth sets the capstone of intruders' transgressions. First, it is the greatest manifestation of their boasting:

It does not merely misidentify external appearances as being worthy of honor but goes beyond even that which is true. As a puffed-up peacock's feathers extend glamorously above its head, the super-apostles' boasts reach far beyond limit. Second, this is the greatest manifestation of their false apostleship. They do not merely claim to have authority from Christ but even claim to do the exact work Christ commissioned Paul to do.

Conclusion

Paul condemns the super-apostles' reception of support because they accept it as payment, setting themselves up as church planters owed by their converts. Conversely, he condones the Jerusalem apostles' reception of support because they accept it as colabor.

At this point, the dorean principle has resolved four apparent discrepancies in Paul's disposition toward financial support. In the next chapter, we will broaden our exploration to see that this fundraising ethic is not merely showcased in a few edge cases of apostolic ministry but pervades the whole of the New Testament and even appears in the Old Testament.

9

The Pattern of Colabor

Theory vs. Practice

As I sit here writing, I just returned from a restaurant that serves plant-based burgers they claim have comparable taste to their real beef. I ordered one of each and conducted a blind taste test with my wife and daughter.

In theory, plant-based meat substitutes seem like a great idea. Plants are more readily available than animals, so they should be cheaper. Vegetables offer a better balance of nutrients than meat for modern diets, so they should be healthier. Recent products using heme (a molecule found in blood) even promise to capture the exact same taste.

Yet all that theory immediately broke down in practice. My wife and daughter immediately identified the impostor with no hesitation. Indeed, I was not convinced by the taste either. More than that, the plant burger was more expensive, and most research these days shows that plant-based meat substitutes are significantly worse for you than traditional, get-it-from-a-farm, fire-it-up-on-the-grill meat.

So far in this book, we've largely discussed theory. We've looked at some of Jesus's and Paul's statements, but we have yet to see the dorean principle at play over the larger scope of Scripture. Does our theory hold together in practice like rich, grass-fed beef, or does it immediately fall apart like a bean burger?

Scripture is brimming with relevant texts, but in this chapter, I
would like us to walk through some of the more prominent examples
we see of colabor. Taking one example from the Old Testament and
several from the New, I'm hoping you will agree with me that not
only do we have didactic statements illustrating this truth from Christ
and his most prolific apostle, but we also have a rich cache of evidence
to reinforce their statements.

Elijah and Elisha

Among Old Testament narratives, the ministries of Elijah and Elisha
stand out as particular examples of colabor. Certainly, there are others,
such as the sacrifices and tithes we examined in Chapter 3. However,
unlike the ministries of most Old Testament prophets and priests, the
ministries of Elijah and Elisha were not limited to the nation of Israel.
In this Gentile setting, we can see their reception of colabor paired
with an explicit rejection of reciprocity. Like a diamond set on black
velvet, the help they receive shines lustrously when held against the
backdrop of refused finances.

The ministries of Elijah and Elisha are marked by the support
of women who understood the importance of using hospitality as
a way to promote the ministry of the word of God. In the case of
Elijah, God instructs the widow of Zarephath to provide for Elijah
while he instructs Elijah to receive the widow's hospitality (1 Kings
17:8–9). She gives out of her poverty, even offering her last bit of food
(1 Kings 17:11–12). Similarly, Elisha receives the sacrificial hospitality of
the Shunammite (2 Kings 4:8–10), recognizing the difficulty involved
(2 Kings 4:13). It might seem like a fair exchange since both of these
women receive back their dead (1 Kings 17:17–24; 2 Kings 4:18–37).
However, in both cases, the giving precedes the miracles, demonstrating that neither participated in an exchange or out of a sense of direct
obligation. Instead, their primary obligation is toward the Lord who
commanded them.

Elisha, continuing on in Elijah's spirit (2 Kings 2:9), miraculously
heals Naaman's leprosy, leading to his apparent conversion. Yet, de-

spite the Syrian commander's urgings, he rejects his gift with a solemn oath.

> Then he [Naaman] returned to the man of God [Elisha], he and all his company, and he came and stood before him. And he said, "Behold, I know that there is no God in all the earth but in Israel; so accept now a present from your servant." But he said, "As the Lord lives, before whom I stand, I will receive none." And he urged him to take it, but he refused. (2 Kings 5:15–16)

In fact, Elisha rejects Naaman's offering so adamantly that when his servant Gehazi goes afterward to secure the gift, he transfers Naaman's leprosy to him as a generational curse (2 Kings 5:20–27). While this malediction no doubt arises from Gehazi's deceitfulness, Elisha explicitly condemns the nature of such an exchange.

> Was it a time to accept money and garments, olive orchards and vineyards, sheep and oxen, male servants and female servants? (2 Kings 5:26b)

What distinguishes the two women and Naaman? The women operate as colaborers. One is an Israelite, while the other has been specifically commissioned and instructed by God. On the other hand, Naaman is a pagan Gentile (2 Kings 5:1), one who has received the blessing of ministry and seeks an opportunity for unmediated repayment. The two women offer hospitality as colabor, but Naaman's present is an attempt at reciprocity.

Jesus's Entourage

Jumping ahead to the New Testament, the disciples accepted support from other Jews living in the towns they visited (Luke 10:5–8). However, many also followed Jesus and his disciples, supporting them materially.

> Soon afterward he went on through cities and villages, proclaiming and bringing the good news of the kingdom of God. And the twelve were with him, and also

some women who had been healed of evil spirits and infirmities: Mary, called Magdalene, from whom seven demons had gone out, and Joanna, the wife of Chuza, Herod's household manager, and Susanna, and many others, who provided for them out of their means. (Luke 8:1–3)

These women colabor with the disciples. While they may occasionally assist more directly in ministry, they help most significantly through their financial contributions. As Luke records, they have been healed by Christ and act out of thankfulness, but we should not label this expression of gratitude as repayment or ministerial reciprocity. Instead, they aim to colabor, supporting the ongoing work of ministry.

Lydia

In Chapter 4, I pointed out that the Philippian church partnered with Paul as a congregation. I'd now like you to consider Lydia, a particular Philippian who partnered with him as an individual. After the apostle's instruction, Lydia embraces Christianity. She offers her hospitality to Paul, and surprisingly, he accepts.

And on the Sabbath day we went outside the gate to the riverside, where we supposed there was a place of prayer, and we sat down and spoke to the women who had come together. One who heard us was a woman named Lydia, from the city of Thyatira, a seller of purple goods, who was a worshiper of God. The Lord opened her heart to pay attention to what was said by Paul. And after she was baptized, and her household as well, she urged us, saying, "If you have judged me to be faithful to the Lord, come to my house and stay." And she prevailed upon us. (Acts 16:14–15)

If Paul refuses support from new converts, why does he receive from Lydia? Prior to her conversion, Scripture describes her as a "worshiper of God," indicating that she already affirmed the true faith through Judaism.

The dorean principle explains Paul's hesitation as well as his eventual acceptance. He does not immediately receive Lydia's hospitality because she may desire to repay him. However, as a worshiper of God who frequents a place of prayer on the Sabbath, she already has some place within the fellowship of God. Paul does not condition Lydia's assistance on the timing of his visit but on her willingness to serve the Lord. She understands the apostle's concerns and appeals to him according to her status as a colaborer: "If you have judged me to be faithful."

The Hosts of Corinth

So far, we've determined that Paul limits his rejection of Corinthian funds to the context of reciprocity. Outside of this context, he willingly accepts support. For example, we've noted that Paul states his eagerness to receive *propempo* support, but as he discovers ready Corinthian colaborers, he receives from them as well.

While planting the church in Corinth, Paul receives help from others like Lydia, those who already belonged to the fellowship of God. First, he stays with Aquila and Priscilla, fellow Jews (Acts 18:2). Soon after, he stays with Titius Justus, a "worshiper of God" who lived next to the synagogue (Acts 18:7). Since Paul established the church in Corinth, these people undoubtedly converted to Christianity through his ministry. However, they were not converts from pagan religion. The apostle freely receives their help as colabor since he first encountered them as fellow servants of God.

After planting the church, Paul speaks of the hospitality he receives from Gaius, who is "almost certainly"[1] the Gaius of Corinth (Rom. 16:23). Phoebe's status as a patron (Rom. 16:2) indicates that she has supported Paul in Corinth, given that Cenchreae is a port of Corinth, and at least to be identified with the larger region of Achaia.

---

[1] Moo, *The Epistle to the Romans*, 935.

Moreover, Paul spends a winter in Corinth (Acts 20:3, 6; cf. 1 Cor. 16:6),[2] receiving aid from the Corinthians.

These instances of hospitality count as colabor even if none of them are explicitly financial. As long as there is some material provision such as lodging, it fits within the rubric of *support*, which Paul only selectively accepts. Recall that in Thessalonica, Paul did not take anyone's bread without paying for it (2 Thess. 3:8). Recall also that Jesus's command revolved around receiving room and board (Matt. 10:10).

Philemon

In Paul's shortest epistle, he appeals to Philemon to receive Onesimus, a runaway slave, as a Christian brother.

> So if you consider me your partner, receive him as you
> would receive me. If he has wronged you at all, or owes
> you anything, charge that to my account. I, Paul, write
> this with my own hand: I will repay it—to say nothing
> of your owing me even your own self. (Philem. 17–19)

The language of colabor colors this account. Paul calls Philemon a partner, having begun the letter addressing him as a fellow worker (Philem. 1). Describing the affair as a business partnership, he negotiates with Philemon to charge anything owed to him to Paul's own account (Philem. 18).

Paul's appeal to personal debt (Philem. 19) may seem to suggest Philemon's anticipated reception of Onesimus as a transaction indicative of ministerial reciprocity. However, this obligation to Paul is not immediate but mediated through mutual obligation to Christ. In Christ, Philemon must comply (Philem. 8), and it is this relationship that demands he honor Paul with his life. Paul certainly did not die for Philemon, but because Christ died for him, he must respect the minister through whom he heard the gospel (cf. Heb. 13:7). Once again, the

---

[2]Bruce, *The Book of the Acts*, 381–382; Jamieson, Fausset, and Brown, *A Commentary, Critical, Practical, and Explanatory, on the Old and New Testaments*, 3.787.

vertical obligation regulates the horizontal obligation. Additionally, Paul emphasizes the voluntary nature of Philemon's participation (Philem. 8–9, 14), indicating that there is no direct obligation that may be enforced.

Providing Philemon another opportunity to colabor, Paul requests a guest room.

> At the same time, prepare a guest room for me, for I am hoping that through your prayers I will be graciously given to you. (Philem. 22)

In saying "at the same time," this request is not set in the context of a returned favor. Instead, Paul contrasts his presence with Philemon to his present imprisonment.[3] He anticipates that he "will be graciously given" to Philemon, not particularly that Philemon will graciously give to him.

The Generosity of Malta

In Acts, a chief official of Malta named Publius hosts Paul for three days (Acts 28:7). He may simply be a congenial procurator, his Roman name hinting that it may be his job to watch the prisoners.[4] Given the variables at play, we cannot regard this hospitality as either an act of horizontal reciprocity or an act of colabor. Publius's interactions with the apostle at this point seem largely confined to Paul as prisoner rather than Paul as minister.

However, these interactions change after Paul heals Publius's father and many other island residents. At this point, the Maltese grant the apostolic crew great honor and give them whatever they need for their travels (Acts 28:10). Most likely, "honor" indicates this material gift (cf. 2 Tim. 3:5, 17). Paul does not refuse gifts from these Gentiles though he rejects gifts from many others. Why would he accept this support?

While the passage contains no explicit mention of the gospel, the author obviously telescopes the narrative. For example, we have no

---

[3] See Moo, *The Letters to the Colossians and to Philemon*, 436–437.
[4] See Bock, *Acts*, 744.

record that Paul rejected the title of "god" (Acts 28:6), yet he certainly did not accept it. Everywhere else in the gospels and Acts, gospel proclamations accompany miraculous healings, and here we have no reason to anticipate anything different. Therefore, we should almost certainly regard the bulk of the Maltese as converts, and especially given the timing of their aid, we may regard their gifts as colabor designed to alleviate Paul's persecution and assist in his missionary travels.

Gaius

The apostle John offers an example of colabor when he instructs Gaius to support those missionaries who are worthy of support.

> Beloved, it is a faithful thing you do in all your efforts for these brothers, strangers as they are, who testified to your love before the church. You will do well to send them on their journey in a manner worthy of God. For they have gone out for the sake of the name, accepting nothing from the Gentiles. Therefore we ought to support people like these, that we may be fellow workers for the truth. (3 John 5–8)

The word for "send them on their journey" is *propempo*, that same term we have seen Paul use in the context of financial support. Here in this epistle, John identifies the act of giving to such men as colabor, establishing a relationship between "fellow workers." This instruction complements the command in his previous epistle not to partner in the wicked works of false teachers by accepting them into one's home—that is, providing support in the form of room and board (2 John 10–11).

However, more significant to our investigation, John explains what makes these missionaries honorable: "they have gone out for the sake of the name, accepting nothing from the Gentiles." Going out for the sake of the name and accepting nothing from the Gentiles are not two independent accolades. No conjunction distinguishes the two; they must be recognized as linked. Their placement in immediate proximity suggests that they are to be viewed as roughly equivalent statements, accepting nothing being the sum proof that these men have gone out for the sake of the name. That is, the fact that they do not take money demonstrates their sincerity, a lack of ulterior motives.

The term "Gentiles" does not primarily denote ethnicity but a status outside the kingdom of God. John commends the financial support of missionaries from the church in an act of colabor but implicitly condemns as duplicitous the reciprocity that would necessarily characterize a financial gift from unbelievers.

Conclusion

While Scripture explicitly teaches the dorean principle, it also demonstrates it implicitly as well. In the Old Testament, Elijah and Elisha received colabor yet refused reciprocity. In the New Testament, we see Jesus and Paul practice what they preach. We even see this ethic at play in John's instructions to Gaius, where he praises churches partnering with missionaries and denounces receiving money from the subjects of the mission field.

Plant burgers may fail to impress in practice, but the dorean principle stands up to expectations when put to the test. Now that we have looked more broadly at the testimony of Scripture, we will also look more broadly at the testimony of the church, exploring some of its history following the era of the apostles.

10

The Testimony of History

Claim vs. Evidence

In 2008, Tom Biscardi snagged a significant amount of camera time when he claimed that he had discovered the carcass of a sasquatch. Someone had finally found Bigfoot! Except he had not. Rather predictably, the animal turned out to be nothing more than a rubber costume shoved into a freezer.

I suppose there will always be believers in Bigfoot, but I am relatively certain no such creature exists. No one has ever found the beast or captured convincing video of it. What's more, no one has ever found an authentic sasquatch track or even sasquatch droppings. Things that exist leave traces of their existence; it's a simple fact of reality. A claim is only a claim apart from evidence.

Similarly, true apostolic practices leave their mark on the church. If the dorean principle was practiced by the apostles in the first century, we should expect to see traces of this practice in the second century. Even if the church experienced times of radical transition, we should expect to see some evidence of this ethic. I believe that when we look to the pages of history, that is exactly what we find.

In the last chapter, we examined the practice of the dorean principle in the first-century church. In this chapter, we will examine its practice in the following century. After establishing that the second-century church fully embraced this ethic, we will briefly look at how the Protestant Reformation attempted to recapture it.

The *Didache*

Quite possibly the oldest extra-biblical Christian writing, the *Didache* functions as a manual of church practice. Also known as *The Teaching of the Twelve Apostles*, it attempts to capture apostolic doctrine and the practice of the church into an orderly guide. Despite these lofty goals, it draws from Matthew to the exclusion of the other gospels, and possibly to the exclusion of all other New Testament books.[1] This document does not attempt to forge new ground or expand upon previous revelation but only to apply what had already been provided by available Scripture.[2] However, this is largely to our advantage since we have founded our own understanding of biblical fundraising ethics on Matthew 10:8–10. In other words, the *Didache* helps us answer the question, "How did the early church apply Jesus's words in Matthew?"

The *Didache*'s importance stems largely from its early authorship, dating to the mid to late first century.[3] The "primitive simplicity" of the *Didache*'s teaching, as well as its silence on persecution, provide the strongest arguments for a first-century date.[4] However, perhaps the early date should not impress us as much as the respect it garnered from the early church. For example, the early church historian Eusebius lists the *Didache* among true, orthodox writings,[5] and Athanasius, the early theologian who defended the doctrine of Trinity, includes it among books approved for baptismal candidates.[6] Additionally, the *Didache* appears to be referenced by Clement of Alexandria and

---

[1] See Varner, "The Didache's Use of the Old and New Testaments," 130.

[2] In the words of Kurt Niederwimmer, "it is entirely aimed at practical needs and lacks any theoretical or even speculative exposition of Christian belief. The compiler is no 'theologian.'" Niederwimmer, *The Didache*, 2.

[3] See Patterson, "The Legacy of Radical Itinerancy in Early Christianity," 315,315n9.

[4] See Varner, "The Didache's Use of the Old and New Testaments," 129.

[5] See Eusebius, "Church History," 3.25.4,6.

[6] See Athanasius, *Letter 39*, 7.

other early Christian witnesses,[7] Ignatius arguably being among their ranks.[8] This support for the *Didache* confirms that it largely represents the early church's understanding of the practical matters it addresses.

Given this brief overview of the document, we can conclude with some degree of confidence that where the *Didache* offers guidance on ministry fundraising, its instruction emerges from an evaluation of New Testament sources and that its judgments were largely shared by the early second-century church. Further, given its early date, one may reasonably conclude that its prescriptions do not stray far from the practice of the apostolic church. At most, it represents a minor evolution from the original pattern of the church rather than a freshly designed program. With that in mind, we turn to the relevant text.[9]

> Let every apostle, when he cometh to you, be received as the Lord; but he shall not abide more than a single day, or if there be need, a second likewise; but if he abide three days, he is a false prophet. And when he departeth let the apostle receive nothing save bread, until he findeth shelter; but if he ask money, he is a false prophet. ... And whosoever shall say in the Spirit, Give me silver or anything else, ye shall not listen to him; but if he tell you to give on behalf of others that are in want, let no man judge him. (Didache 11.4–6, 12)

Clearly, the *Didache* takes serious precautions against itinerant teachers who would take advantage of the church. In a different context, it labels anyone who wrongly accepts the support of the Christian community a "trafficker in Christ" or "Christ-monger"[10] (Didache 12.5). We may identify several prohibitions here:

1. staying [in a home] for three or more days,

---

[7] See Niederwimmer, *The Didache*, 4–18.

[8] See Jefford, "Did Ignatius of Antioch Know the Didache?"

[9] Unless otherwise noted, all quotations here of the *Didache* and *The Shepherd of Hermas* come from Lightfoot, *The Apostolic Fathers*.

[10] The *Didache* uses the term *christemporos*, a single word combining the Greek words *christos* (Christ) and *emporos* (merchant). "Christ-monger" is the translation provided by Roberts and Donaldson, *The Ante-Nicene Fathers*.

2. taking more than bread for one's journey,
3. asking for money for one's journey, and
4. asking for money under the pretense of divine instruction.

On the surface, several points stand at odds with our conclusions from the former chapters. Benjamin Franklin quipped that fish and visitors stink after three days, but beyond this humorous sentiment, it is not clear why there would be a prohibition against prolonged hospitality, especially if Paul is willing to spend the entire winter with the Corinthians (1 Cor. 16:6). The ban on accepting money for a journey likewise seems out of step with the previously covered notion of *propempo* support.

The confusion arises from the fact that the *Didache* speaks to an established Christian people, yet appears to prohibit them from colaboring. However, clarity arises from recognizing that this paragraph addresses a prophet of questionable veracity (Didache 11.13). Others are to recognize him as a true prophet, in part, by the ethic he exhibits in managing his own support among an unknown people. Prior to such a demonstration, the people should treat him with a healthy caution. Regarding one firmly identified as a true prophet, the *Didache* readily acknowledges that he is "worthy of his food" (Didache 13.1) and deserves the "firstfruit," of money, possessions, etc. (Didache 13.7).

Since we have seen these instructions most clearly pronounced in the epistles of Paul, I find it especially fascinating that the author of the *Didache* apparently arrives at these conclusions apart from a clear knowledge of the apostle's writings.[11] In other words, the *Didache* indicates that Jesus established the dorean principle and that it may be understood in the gospel of Matthew without appealing to any later developments. Prior to Paul's rejection of hospitality when arriving in Corinth, Thessalonica, and Ephesus, the church understood that it is

---

[11] Note, for example, that the *Didache* remarks that a laborer is worthy of his "food" (as in Matthew 10:10), rather than his "wages" (as in 1 Timothy 5:18). In part, a lack of direct reference to the Pauline corpus demonstrates this lack of exposure. See Milavec, *The Didache*, ix. Additionally, the indications of an arid climate suggest a geographic locale removed from the missional territory of Paul. See González, "New Testament Koinónia and Wealth," 224.

unbecoming for a minister of Christ to support himself by receiving direct payment from his converts.[12]

The Shepherd of Hermas

A similar, albeit more specific, concern arises in *The Shepherd of Hermas*. As with the *Didache*, *The Shepherd* is a Christian writing that was widely respected by the early church.[13] Once again, this indicates that its judgments are largely representative of those held by the early church, reflecting the counsel of Scripture.

The Shepherd of Hermas warns against greedy prophets who willingly say anything for the sake of gain (Shepherd 43.2–3,8). As a precautionary measure against such things, it decries private prophecy, demanding that teachers teach plainly and openly, in a Christian assembly (Shepherd 43.13–14). However, perhaps its most direct rebuke of false prophets comes in the form of a condemnation of ministerial reciprocity.

> In the first place, that man who seemeth to have a spirit exalteth himself, and desireth to have a chief place, and straight-way he is impudent and shameless and talkative and conversant in many luxuries and in many other deceits and receiveth money for his prophesying, and if he receiveth not, he prophesieth not. Now can a divine Spirit receive money and prophesy? It is not possible for a prophet of God to do this, but the spirit of such prophets is earthly. (Shepherd 43.12)

In forbidding the *requirement* of remuneration, *The Shepherd* does not clearly prohibit the *acceptance* of remuneration. However, it goes on to say that a divine Spirit cannot "receive money and prophesy." Here, *The Shepherd* offers an unqualified rejection of ministerial

---

[12]Niederwimmer remarks that this embargo on extended hospitality "recalls the prohibitions of Jesus against taking wallet or money on missionary activity." Niederwimmer, *The Didache*, 166–177.

[13]The Muratorian Canon commends *The Shepherd of Hermas* as a useful work. Likewise, Irenaeus, Hippolytus, Ambrose, Jerome, Athanasius, and others reference it positively. See Osiek, *The Shepherd of Hermas*, 4–7.

reciprocity. It rejects as insincere any who would receive in direct exchange for teaching.

Apollonius

Not much is known of Apollonius of Ephesus, but his writings warrant mention for their status as early witnesses to the practices of the church. These writings no longer exist in a complete form, but the early church historian Eusebius recorded his contentions with the heretic Montanus. Of Montanus, Apollonius reports,

> This is he who... appointed collectors of money; who contrived the receiving of gifts under the name of offerings; who provided salaries for those who preached his doctrine, that its teaching might prevail through gluttony.[14]

Clearly, Apollonius opposes greedy accumulation of wealth, although it is less clear why he objects to salaries in particular. It seems likely that he protests the nature of the commission: pay offered in return for preaching. Regardless, it is plain that Apollonius opposes prophets accepting gifts in the context of their ministry.

> Does not all Scripture seem to you to forbid a prophet to receive gifts and money? When therefore I see the prophetess [Prisca] receiving gold and silver and costly garments, how can I avoid reproving her? ... If they deny that their prophets have received gifts, let them acknowledge this: that if they are convicted of receiving them, they are not prophets.[15]

Notably, Apollonius appeals to Christ as he promotes his ethic.

> For although the Lord said, "Provide neither gold, nor silver, neither two coats," these men, in complete opposition, transgress in respect to the possession of the forbidden things. For we will show that those whom

---

[14] Eusebius, "Church History," 5.18.2.
[15] Ibid., 5.18.4,11.

they call prophets and martyrs gather their gain not only
from rich men, but also from the poor, and orphans,
and widows.[16]

Depending on how we understand Apollonius, one could argue
that he strays from the dorean principle, rejecting all financial support for ministers rather than merely rejecting ministerial reciprocity.
However, congregational support has always been a common feature
in churches, even in the first and second centuries. For Apollonius
to take particular issue with Montanus, the false prophet's practice
must have deviated beyond the typical practice, possessing a more
commercial character.

Regardless, Apollonius appeals to the common understanding
of the church and points to some divergent practice in the sect of
Montanus. Whether Apollonius's biblical understanding is accurate
or not, it represents a second-century Christian mindset, which was
formed and influenced by first-century Christian practices. In other
words, even apart from perfect agreement, these objections to payment
confirm the second-century church affirmed something akin to the
dorean principle.

Those familiar with church history might know that in the course
of his contending against Montanus, Apollonius incurred the rebuke
of Tertullian, one of the most important second-century theologians.
But on this point, the two were agreed. As Tertullian writes, "There
is no buying and selling of any sort in the things of God."[17]

Martin Luther

Flash forward to the Protestant Reformation. In the first three centuries of the church, we see the ripples and echoes of the dorean
principle in play, but the sixteenth century concerns us for an altogether different reason. The eventual corruption of the church had
led to a degradation in fundraising practices. Rather than having the
opportunity to maintain the apostolic practice, the Reformers found

---

[16]Ibid., 5.18.7.
[17]Tertullian, "Apology," 39.

themselves saddled with the task of restoring a biblical view of money. In fact, while the Reformation centered around the doctrines of Scripture and salvation, the relationship between money and ministry was arguably the primary catalyst of the Reformation.

In the early sixteenth century, the sale of indulgences—reductions on time spent in purgatory—financed the construction of St. Peter's Basilica in the Vatican. In Germany, this effort was led by Johann Tetzel, a friar whose marketing skills have been immortalized in the following couplet:

> *As soon as a coin in the coffer rings,*
> *A soul from purgatory to heaven springs.*

German priest Martin Luther (1483–1546) objected to this commercial treatment of salvation, and on October 31, 1517, he nailed his 95 Theses against the sale of indulgences to the door of All Saints' Church in Wittenberg. This act of defiance sparked the Protestant Reformation, the largest religious and cultural revolution the Western world has ever experienced.

Luther believed a minister was obligated to be selfless in his office and saw the calling of pastor to be one of imitation of Christ in his sacrifice. Concerning the pope, he writes, "Is it not his duty to do all that he can for all Christians without reward, solely for God's sake, nay, even to shed his blood for them?"[18] He goes as far as to say that a ministry endeavor that seeks to raise money lacks the marks of divine approval: "As we see, every project of men bears money; the Word of God bears nothing but the cross."[19] Of course, Luther also believed ministers should receive regular support in order to sustain the proclamation of the gospel.[20]

On one hand, it seems clear that Luther roughly affirmed the dorean principle, denying that the message of salvation should be sold and affirming that congregants should support their ministers. However, his writings never ventured much further than a rebuke of extremes. Other figures in the Protestant Reformation voiced similar

---

[18] Luther, *First Principles of the Reformation*, 69.

[19] Plass, *What Luther Says*, 1016.

[20] See Luther, *A Commentary on St. Paul's Epistle to the Galatians*, 237–238.

concerns, but in my estimation, none ever made it quite as far as to articulate a robust ethic distinguishing the wrongful and rightful receipt of money in ministry.

Conclusion

Looking back on the pages of history, we see that the second-century church maintained the apostolic practice of the dorean principle. Moreover, they understood this ethic to be a Scriptural precept, defending it largely from the gospel of Matthew. Unlike Bigfoot, the teaching of the dorean principle in the first-century church left traces in the following century that corroborate its prevalence among the churches founded by the apostles.

Later, after centuries of increased disregard in the church at large, the Reformers recognized the need to restore a biblical ethic of ministry fundraising. By and large, they determined that Scripture forbids the sale of ministry and yet commands the support of ministers. However, these Reformers were largely satisfied to counter the extremes of greed and neglect. The work begun at the time of the Reformation remains in need of completion. For those who wish to take up that mantle, I believe that the dorean principle holds the keys to properly articulating the biblical ethic and putting it into practice.

11

The Scope of Ministry

Impunity vs. Jurisdiction

One morning on the way to my high school, I was listening to the host of a radio show recount the story of a woman who led a band of police officers on a high-speed chase. Racing down the interstate, she eventually exited and led the authorities through a suburban area. Surprisingly, she neither crashed nor pulled over in surrender. Instead, she peeled into the driveway of her home and ran inside.

What is it that caused the woman to do this? The radio host accepted answers from callers. Did she have a medical emergency? Did she need to use her bathroom? The first caller answered correctly: She believed she could not be arrested on her own property. However, as the woman learned when the strong arm of the law forcibly entered her home, that is not how police jurisdiction works.

Similarly, many imagine that within their own class of ministry, they may operate with impunity, outside any kind of stipulations. However, just as the Lord reigns over all the earth, the jurisdiction of the dorean principle extends to all gospel ministries.

In this chapter, I want to explore the boundaries of this jurisdiction in the context of the church. By offering practical application, we will reify the ethic put forward in previous chapters, but I also want to give it shape by attempting to sketch its limitations.

Because we will be referring to this principle more frequently from here to the end of the book, I'll restate our biblical ethic of ministry fundraising one more time before we continue.

> *In the context of gospel proclamation, accepting support as anything other than an act of colabor compromises the sincerity of ministry.*

Now let's embark on the journey of practical application!

Defining Gospel Ministry

The dorean principle begins with the phrase, "in the context of gospel ministry." Given that our stated principle looks to regulate the work of ministry, we must ask what exactly *ministry* is and how far its scope extends. Some recent attempts to understand vocation in light of the Bible bridge the secular/sacred divide between the work of ministers and laymen.[1] While such attempts may have merit in seeing God's calling for all walks of life, this blurring of distinctions can only provide confusion for our purposes of defining boundaries. There must be some activities that are particularly *ministry* and some that are discernibly *not ministry*. Otherwise, our principle would reject *all* commercial exchanges.

As a starting point, the apostle Paul's concerns regarding ministry fundraising revolve around the proclamation of the gospel (1 Cor. 9:18; 2 Cor. 11:7). We may therefore begin by qualifying our considerations, limiting them particularly to *gospel* ministry. In other words, the dorean principle concerns the explicit proclamation of the word of God rather than other forms of charitable service, which may be too broad to warrant regulation.

However, we should pause given that Christ's command extends beyond preaching, including miraculous healings among those things which should not be offered for a price (Matt. 10:8). In context, the purpose of those miraculous healings is to demonstrate the veracity of the good news (Matt. 10:7). Even here, the gospel is still in view.

---

[1] For example, see Keller, *Every Good Endeavor*, 67–71.

Certain types of service, like miracle-working, have such a relationship to that message, that while the gospel may be proclaimed apart from them, they cannot rightly exist divorced from the proclamation of the gospel.

For our purposes, gospel ministry is *any activity that proclaims the gospel or directly attends to its proclamation*.

Though not immediately obvious, this includes all religious instruction. From a biblical standpoint, the goal of any Christian teaching is not to stand on its own but ultimately to communicate the gospel (1 Cor. 2:2; Heb. 6:1). Consequently, the dorean principle regulates teaching in many formats and contexts. From sermons to books, both live and recorded formats lie in its purview. From Sunday school to seminary, it governs contexts both within and outside the regular operations of the church.

Accepting Support

The dorean principle speaks of support and its acceptance. Within the category of "acceptance," we may define three modes: *requirement*, *request*, and *receipt*. Each forms a concentric circle within the other: those who require support are willing to request and receive it, and those who request support are willing to receive it. The dorean principle forbids each one outside the context of colabor but identifies each inner circle as more problematic than the preceding.

Requirement: Most clear among the three, a minister cannot require support in exchange for ministry. To hold ministry hostage for a ransom would make one a free agent rather than a servant with a charge from his master. Rather than requiring repayment, a godly minister should, like Paul, be willing to spend and be spent (2 Cor. 12:15).

Request: Beyond requiring payment, the dorean principle prohibits requesting anything in exchange for ministry. Such a request implies a direct obligation to give in exchange for the service rendered. Voluntary payment is still payment, not colabor.

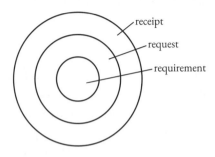

Figure 11.1: Three Modes of Accepting Support

Receipt: Finally, ministers ought not receive in exchange for ministry. Many imagine that unsolicited gifts should be free from scrutiny, but even that which was not requested may constitute reciprocity.

Of course, all these prohibitions hinge on the phrase "in exchange for ministry." That is, they only forbid reciprocity, not colabor. One may receive colabor, even request it, since such a request does not impose a direct obligation but appeals to divine obligation. Additionally, one may even *require* colabor for ministry, voluntarily abstaining from ministry as determined by financial need. For example, in Corinth, Paul refrained from full-time ministry and instead labored to support himself. When fellow evangelists from Macedonia arrived, presumably with financial relief (cf. Phil. 4:15), Paul resumed full-time ministry (Acts 18:5). Jesus even commanded his disciples only to go where they would have support to do the work of ministry (Matt. 10:14). In these circumstances, money is a means rather than an end.

Ministerial Staff

Considering the dorean principle in the life of the church gives us an opportunity to evaluate how we think about weekly financial contributions. First, the congregation ought not be misled about the nature of their giving. Rather than being taught that they owe ministers directly, they should be taught that they owe it to God to support his ministers, especially those from whom they have benefited. Beyond this, they should understand that their giving is an act of colabor. In the words of D. A. Carson, "the church does not pay its ministers; rather it provides them with resources so that they are able to serve freely."[2] The congregation works together with their minister to ensure the gospel is proclaimed. As such, it moves the charitable act from a negative center to a positive center, from the canceling of debt owed to investment in the kingdom of heaven. Not only does a right understanding of giving correct an erring ethic, but it also has the power to enliven the giver.

Of course, ministers also should recognize the nature of their income. To quote another prominent theologian, "Christian ministers should refuse remuneration for the sake of the gospel. When Christians accept money for ministry, they ought never view it as a wage but a gift."[3] While the distinction between "wage" and "gift" might differ from our chosen vocabulary of "reciprocity" and "colabor," the concerns coincide.

Sermons

Naturally, preaching ministries should offer sermons at no charge. Few churches, if any, have a turnstile at the door, but it was not that long ago that many charged pew rents. Moreover, with the rise of technology, sermons have been sold in print and digital form for some time. As just one prominent example, an archive of Tim Keller's sermons currently costs $1,600, marked down from a list price of $3,300.[4]

In contrast to these commercial practices, the church should engage in the free proclamation of the gospel, not only by permitting visitors to freely enter the building for worship services but also by

---

[2]Carson, *When Jesus Confronts the World*, 142.
[3]Blomberg, *Matthew*, 171.
[4]Gospel in Life, *Tim Keller MP3 Sermon Archive*.

providing any recordings freely. Most churches already practice this, sharing their sermons freely on sites such as Sermon Audio.

Honorariums do not violate this ethic but should be regarded as a fruitful means of supporting interim preachers and teachers. If the purpose of a church is to gather for the collective worship of God in the preaching and hearing of the word, the congregation and preacher work toward the same end. Anchored by a mutual desire to properly honor God, a church provides an honorarium as an act of colabor. If a regular preacher receives from his church in coordination with his labors among them, then a visiting preacher may do the same. Thus, Peter was able to arrive at Corinth and receive financial support for his work there (cf. 1 Cor. 9:5).

Special Services

Irregular religious worship services warrant special scrutiny. Any amount of religious instruction, including worship leading, should be offered without pay. Such charges are not unheard of in modern times. For example, the church pastored by the then president of the Southern Baptist Convention charged for entry to their 2019 "Good Friday Worship" service.[5]

Frequently, special worship events run outside the context of a church, under the auspices of a concert or conference. Such affairs typically charge not only to recuperate physical costs but also to fund religious instruction. Ticket sales that fail to identify the exact objects of purchase—food? music? a message?—along with a blurring between worship and entertainment, threaten to transgress the dorean principle.

Our concerns regarding special services extend to weddings, funerals, and even counseling. Unlike typical teaching or worship services, these tend to focus on a particular party: the newlyweds, the family of the deceased, or the counselee. In these circumstances, the needs of the few rise to the forefront, and an exchange of money suggests that it is offered in return for the gospel ministry provided in that context.

---

[5] The Summit Church, *Easter at the Summit*.

Not only should churches and ministers refrain from advertising a fee; they should also not accept one. As already stated, honorariums do not necessarily violate our stated principle, but where money changes hands between one in need of a service and one who provides it, is it clear that gospel ministry is not being purchased?

Conceivably, one could give as an act of colabor at a special service, but the context suggests that any such money would constitute a direct payment. Nothing apparent distinguishes a check proffered to a counseling pastor and a check proffered to a secular therapist. The ambiguity of the situation typically places the minister in a position where he cannot discern the intent of the individual and accept money responsibly. Such a minister ought to, like Paul, simply refuse funds in situations that suggest direct repayment and look forward to accepting support in less compromising circumstances.

The Importance of Context

As we've seen, context indicates a financial exchange as reciprocity or colabor. For example, in the context of a church plant, Paul rejects Corinthian funds as reciprocity (1 Cor. 9:15). In the context of being sent out to other regions, he gladly receives them (1 Cor. 16:6).

Several aspects of context may indicate the nature of a contribution, but chief among these are language and/or earmarking. For example, using the language of colabor, a ministry might advertise, "You've seen our impact; please consider partnering with us." By employing the terminology of "partnership," this call to action indicates that any who give join in laboring for the Lord, bringing their resources into a common pool for a common purpose. However, a ministry might solicit donations with the following appeal: "You've benefited from our teaching, please consider giving back." This language of reciprocity suggests a direct obligation to man rather than an indirect obligation mediated by God. Similarly, "suggested donations" offer a clever attempt at relieving one of the notion of obligation but almost certainly earmark a contribution as repayment.

Opposition and Boycotts

The dorean principle stands at odds with much gospel proclamation as it exists in the world. While inconsistency on this point may indicate false teaching,[6] true teachers also adopt compromised practices, unaware of the implications. Should we oppose or boycott such ministries to promote a biblical ethic? Thankfully, the apostle Paul gives a rather direct answer. Observing that some preach Christ "not sincerely," he responds,

> What then? Only that in every way, whether in pretense or in truth, Christ is proclaimed, and in that I rejoice. (Phil. 1:18)

Along with Paul, we should rejoice at the gospel efforts of those who preach truly but not as sincerely as they ought. Antagonistic pursuits such as boycotts are not only unnecessary but also largely unhelpful, and it would be unwise to intentionally cut oneself off from the vast array of biblical teaching offered at a cost.

Similar to boycotts, one may circumvent paywalls that restrict access to ministry—e.g., via illicit downloads. If the gospel is the Lord's to offer and ministers are not permitted to sell their teaching, such behavior may seem justified. In considering the temple tax, Jesus offers a nuanced response to unjust financial impositions attached to spiritual blessings.

> "What do you think, Simon? From whom do kings of the earth take toll or tax? From their sons or from others?" And when he said, "From others," Jesus said to him, "Then the sons are free. However, not to give offense to them, go to the sea and cast a hook and take the first fish that comes up, and when you open its mouth you will find a shekel. Take that and give it to them for me and for yourself." (Matt. 17:25b–27)

Having a right to the benefits of the temple, the disciples do not owe the tax to those who collect it. However, for the sake of peace, it is often best to bear such burdens.

---

[6]See Chapter 7.

Conclusion

The dorean principle offers a foundation from which we can begin to concretize the New Testament model of ministry fundraising. In the next chapters, we will explore more specifics, beginning with the relationship between the dorean principle and parachurch ministry.

12

The Challenge of Parachurch

Help vs. Hurt

Nothing makes for an exciting hero like a vigilante. Fed up with the inefficiencies or corruptions of governing authorities, a zealous hero goes outside the purview of the law to take matters of justice into his own hands. He captures and punishes criminals, unencumbered by red tape and crooked bureaucrats. Fueled by righteous indignation, he restores order in the world. It's no wonder fictional characters like Robin Hood and Batman garner mass appeal.

In reality, however, vigilante justice is often problematic. Rarely guided by a careful weighing of the matter, psychological instability or mob mentality typically provokes such activity. Even those who do operate with some sense of rationality frequently commit grave errors by abandoning the safeguards of civil government. There is a reason the phrase "kangaroo court" does not ring with positive connotations.

In a sense, the church has her own set of vigilantes. When Jesus established God's heavenly kingdom on earth, he decided to operate through a franchise of local institutions he called "the church," assemblies constituted with particular offices and functions. Many have found this structure inefficient, opting to establish their own institutions to accomplish religious ends, widely known as *parachurch* organizations. Many of these ministries may be accompanied by the excitement of fictional vigilantes, but they often encounter problems similar to the ones faced by real-world vigilantes.

I don't write all this to challenge the legitimacy of parachurch ministries but to call attention to the fact that they introduce their own complications, especially when it comes to ministry fundraising. Since they cannot rely on the fundraising practice of the church, they tend to create new avenues of support that potentially violate the dorean principle. In this chapter, I would like to offer a quick overview of where exactly the issues lie, and how a healthy focus on the local church may circumvent them.

Church Identity vs. Parachurch Identity

The church is that body of believers Christ instituted to represent his kingdom on earth. The *universal church* is composed of all Christians everywhere while the *local church* refers to a particular society of Christians characterized by their regular gathering for worship.

Etymologically, "para" indicates coming alongside something. *Parachurch ministry* is simply any ministry regulated outside of the local church whose primary goal is to aid the church, whether local or universal. Thus, while the label is typically used for organizations like InterVarsity Christian Fellowship or Compassion International, broadly it applies even to individuals operating outside the structure of the local church with the intent to serve the church.

Church Structure vs. Parachurch Structure

The essential distinction between the local church and the parachurch lies in structure. Understanding this distinction is the key to recognizing the potential pitfalls of parachurch entities, especially as related to the dorean principle. Let's look at this structure according to the Bible's breakdown of a church: the congregation, elders, and deacons.

The congregation is the membership of a church. While some churches do not practice formal membership, there is generally an understanding of who is permitted to participate in the Lord's supper on a regular basis. The congregation ultimately forms the primary source of accountability in the church. Even if the church does not practice congregational voting, the people vote with their feet, joining and supporting those ministries which operate as they see fit. Parachurch ministries rarely have similarly defined membership, or even similarly defined goals.

The elders of a church watch over a congregation, managing the teaching of the church and leading it in discerning doctrinal issues. Ideally, a body of elders would consider church fundraising practices in light of the word of God with especially discerning eyes. Parachurch organizations typically guarantee no such oversight.

The deacons of a church have authority over the physical resources of the church to meet the physical needs of the church. The Bible requires they conform to the standards set in 1 Timothy 3:8–13. Outside the church, those who take on similar roles may be vetted spiritually but are rarely assessed by the same rubric.

In each example, a secular position replaces a sacred one. The structure that protects the ethical collection of resources in the church rarely exists in other organizations, nor can it ever completely. In adding such church structures, a parachurch organization would cease to exist as such and would simply become a church.

Church Fundraising vs. Parachurch Fundraising

The Bible establishes a model of fundraising for the church: the voluntary contributions of the congregation. Presuming they are offered in an effort to colabor with the church, they perfectly accord with the dorean principle.

We see these contributions first in Acts, where the people pool their resources (Acts 2:44–45) to be distributed by the apostles, functioning as elders (Acts 4:34–35), and later a body known as "the seven," functioning as deacons (Acts 6:1–6). Elsewhere, Paul commands the church in Corinth to contribute weekly on the first day of every week (1 Cor. 16:1–2).

In contrast, the Bible prescribes no source of income for parachurch organizations. Consequently, the exigencies of ministry drive them toward innovative fundraising practices, frequently creating opportunities to transgress the dorean principle. While not exclusive to parachurch institutions, there is a reason the sale of ministry occurs more frequently outside the church than inside the church. Book sales cover author commission, conference tickets cover speaker fees, tuition payments cover tenured salaries, and proprietary licenses cover musician paychecks. Yet by and large, the voluntary contributions of the congregation suffice for church-employed ministers.

Alternative Approaches

Parachurch entities typically form for the sake of expediency, the alternatives deemed too inefficient or ineffective. However, in light of the dorean principle, we should consider several alternatives to the practices of parachurch ministries. Moving from more to less aggressive measures, the following three strategies provide potential replacements for standard parachurch practices that abandon the dorean principle.

Conducting ministry under the auspices of the local church: Many parachurch endeavors could directly translate to church endeavors. Such ministry would be subject to the authority structure of the church and receive its funding directly from the church. The governance of a parachurch entity that seems too large or has too many stakeholders to fit within a single church could potentially be subdivided or franchised to be run by multiple churches.

This would work for many sophisticated organizations, but it would work especially well for ministries of individuals. For pastors and other staff, churches could recognize their special labor in their regular salary. In the case of others, nothing inhibits the church from creating a position for them. For example, some churches have a "scholar in residence" position that could be appropriately compensated. Christian authors who produce valuable teaching ought to be supported so that they have the liberty to write without fearing the financial ramifications of abandoning their day job.

However, a number of Christian authors write and publish books independent of the authority structure and financing of their church. In the end, they frequently support their work by selling their finished product, some even priding themselves for doing so. To draw examples from the spectrum of evangelicalism, Rick Warren and Joel Osteen have both opted out of taking any income from their churches, instead living primarily on book royalties.[1] However, this swaps colabor with reciprocity, reversing the dorean principle. They proudly reject colabor and happily accept reciprocity. The church that wishes to colabor with the minister should be permitted to do so, and none should be asked to purchase ministry through book sales or otherwise. In contrast, some have commendably offered their works for free, rejecting royalties from hard copy sales, living only on the support provided by their churches. John Piper is an example of one such minister.[2]

Fundraising through church partnerships: Those parachurch organizations which receive their funding largely from individuals could limit their solicitations to established churches. By receiving money from churches that wish to partner with them, they would rely only on the voluntary contribution of congregations rather than the sale of religious instruction.

Prefunding: Rather than attempting to recoup costs after the fact via ticket and literature sales, parachurch organizations could prefund their ministry. For example, religious conference organizers could work with churches and individuals to collect money to support the teachers rather than doing so through ticket sales. Similarly, rather than relying on book sales, Christian publishing houses could work with churches and individuals to establish a joint fund from which

---

[1]Laura, *Pastor Rick Warren Is Well Prepared For A Purpose Driven Retirement*; Kumar, "Joel Osteen's Lakewood Church Has Annual Budget of $90 Million: Here's How That Money Is Spent."

[2]See Hansen, "Piper on Pastors' Pay."

authors would be paid. Instead of one entity shouldering all the risk and potentially turning a financial profit, many believers would partner together in sharing the risk, praying together for a spiritual harvest.

Crowdfunding utilities such as Kickstarter or Patreon offer a viable alternative to the work-first, receive-later model of the publishing industry. With these tools, one may receive funds from partners on a regular basis or raise money for a ministry endeavor prior to commencing. These approaches would give Christian ministers a way to raise support from those genuinely interested in supporting the ministry without appealing directly to those who are the main targets of the ministry. However, a word of caution: crowdfunding utilities often encourage offering perks at different donation levels. In the context of ministry, such seeming bribery does not accord with the dorean principle.

Seminaries

As a case study, a particular category of parachurch organizations applies here. Seminaries typically operate outside of the direct oversight of the local church but have significant impact on the church at large.

While financial aid programs exist, rarely does one complete a seminary degree apart from incurring substantial costs. As an example, Reformed Theological Seminary presently charges tuition at typical rates. At $585 per semester hour,[3] for a 106-hour Master of Divinity degree,[4] that totals to $62,010, not counting the additional host of fees that go beyond raw tuition. Given that seminary education constitutes religious instruction in nearly the purest sense, the dorean principle demands that seminaries not accept money from their students in exchange. However, rather than destroying these institutions, several options compatible with the dorean principle offer ways to preserve them.

---

[3]RTS, *Tuition and Fees.*
[4]RTS, *Master of Divinity.*

Rather than raising money through tuition, seminaries could be funded by individuals and churches looking to support the work of the school. For example, such an institution does not have to directly salary their instructors but could instead provide a framework for churches to support them. These issues of staff largely exhaust our concerns since the dorean principle does not necessarily regulate student room and board. For brick and mortar seminaries, compliance with the biblical ethic may largely reside in delineating facility costs from staff costs, ensuring the latter is funded through responsibly sourced donations.

However, the advent of online seminaries offers a new way forward with little concern for physical resources. In fact, several of these seminaries have adopted a similar model, with virtually all faculty receiving no compensation directly from the seminary. For example, The Log College and Seminary and Forge Theological Seminary both provide free educations through removing the financial burden of a physical campus, choosing educational material that minimizes costs, and relying on the support of volunteer faculty. These individuals often receive support for their work from their own churches, who understand their academic efforts to be an aspect of their ministry. By structuring themselves this way, these institutions relegate spiritual formation and other time-intensive aspects of seminary life to the local church.

While this trend represents a radical shift from the traditional model, it promotes the primacy of the local church and, consequently, compliance with the dorean principle. As more seminaries follow this model, we may hope that free education will become the norm in pastoral training.

Conferences

As an additional case study, gospel-themed conferences likewise collect large sums of money from attendees. Not uncommonly, organizers sell tickets at a cost approximating $100 a day. For example, Together for the Gospel's T4G20 was a three-day exclusive livestream event with registration costing $299.[5] At thousands in attendance, this represents over $1 million in ticket sales. If the purpose of such events is truly to promote the gospel, then the dorean principle must shape its commerce.

Naturally, large events require substantial sums of money to reserve venues, print conference materials, etc. Thus, it is not surprising that fees are often associated with conference attendance. However, according to our ethic, one should not charge for the actual ministry of the gospel. A key issue here is that in conference tickets, material costs are rarely delineated from the cost of the instruction itself. When they are, it becomes apparent whether the organizers intend to sell religious instruction to the audience. For example, in order to avoid the suggestion that the teaching itself is being sold, a ticket could be labeled a "meal and facilities pass." Regardless, our ethic also regulates all that directly attends to the proclamation of the word, so gospel-centric event organizers should consider finding willing colaborers rather than charging for attendance.

Conclusion

Because parachurch ministry lacks the structure of the church, it opens itself to additional opportunities to violate the dorean principle. Most notably, it lacks the regular contributions of the saints and so frequently resorts to creative fundraising measures. These measures often cross the line set by the dorean principle.

Recognizing the tacit dangers of parachurch ministry, we should respond proactively, finding ways to generate support through colabor rather than reciprocity. Where possible, we should even consider restructuring parachurch activities under the auspices of the church.

---

[5] Together for the Gospel, *Together for the Gospel*.

13

The Issue of Copyright

Protection vs. Freedom

In the mid-sixth century, an Irish monk named Finnian traveled home from Rome. Excitement gripped him, for he had come in possession of a great treasure: a Bible. While he certainly had access to some Scripture in his hometown, this Bible represented a purer and more complete copy than anything he owned, and all in a single volume. Nearby monks heard of Finnian's new prize, and many came from significant distances to see it. It more than pleased Finnian to show it off, yet all the same, he was rather possessive of his book.

Among those who visited was a monk named Colmcille, a charismatic, young redhead. He was equally excited by the Bible, so much, in fact, that he sneaked into the church where it was kept in order to spend the night copying it. He administered a scriptorium nearby and anticipated the opportunity to reproduce and disseminate the Scriptures on a grander scale. When Finnian discovered the act taking place, he became furious. Soon afterward, he pursued litigation.

Both men requested an audience before the High King Diarmaid for arbitration, each one confident that justice would rule in his favor. Finnian argued that because the book was his, the copy was his as well. Colmcille responded, offering his defense.

> My friend's claim seeks to apply a worn out law to a new reality. Books are different to other chattels (possessions)

and the law should recognize this. Learned men like us, who have received a new heritage of knowledge through books, have an obligation to spread that knowledge, by copying and distributing those books far and wide. I haven't used up Finnian's book by copying it. He still has the original and that original is none the worse for my having copied it. Nor has it decreased in value because I made a transcript of it. The knowledge in books should be available to anybody who wants to read them and has the skills or is worthy to do so; and it is wrong to hide such knowledge away or to attempt to extinguish the divine things that books contain.[1]

To Colmcille's shock, the king ruled in Finnian's favor. Many speculations surround this event. Perhaps it represented an unbiased attempt at justice, or perhaps the court counselor, a druid, sought to hinder the advancement of Christianity. Regardless, the details of the story certainly make for interesting considerations.[2]

In our day, access to efficient copying is vastly more widespread than it was in Colmcille's. Through the digitization of information, even a child can reproduce a book in near-infinitesimal time at near-infinite quantities. Through the internet, that same work may be disseminated to nearly every person on the planet. If the fiery monk worried that outdated laws would hinder the advancement of the gospel in a new era, how much more should we revisit those same concerns?

Defined broadly, copyright is any legal mechanism that regulates the reproduction and use of creative works.[3] While copyright offers legal protections to authors, it simultaneously restricts the freedoms of those who consume creative works. In this chapter, I would like to comment on how the dorean principle should shape our view of

---

[1] Corrigan, "Colmcille and the Battle of the Book," 6.

[2] See ibid.

[3] Misinformation often clouds popular understanding of copyright. For further clarification, I have provided a brief overview of copyright law in the United States in Appendix B.

its use in ministry and then provide some alternatives for modern ministry workers.[4]

Copyright and Obligation

The conclusions in the previous chapters of this book should lead us to question the church's use of copyright protection mechanisms in the context of gospel ministry. If a minister is to give freely, has he really done so if he retains exclusive rights to the content of his proclamation? In my estimation, the answer is a resounding *no*.

Even though maintaining full copyright protection does not necessitate an exchange of money, it does impose a burden on the recipient of ministry. Apart from express permission, he may not copy, modify, or redistribute that work, the information he has received. Note that this imposes a *requirement*, requirement being the innermost circle of the forms of acceptance that violate the dorean principle. As such, it is the most serious form of violation. Moreover, typically, money *is* involved in the exchange. Ministers refuse ministry—in the form of books, recorded lectures, etc.—apart from a payment collected from the recipient.

Additionally, the involuntary nature of copyright precludes co-labor. One who complies with legal restrictions does not offer a freewill sacrifice to the Lord but only a concession to the one protected by the law. One who gives money to receive access to gospel-related material does so only as an exchange, compensating another to settle a debt owed to him.

Copyright and Sincerity

Stepping back and examining things through the lens of sincerity, we must question the earnestness of one who asserts all copyrights over the content of their ministry. If they impose restrictions or require

---

[4]While the dorean principle leads me to certain conclusions, some theologians have advanced a broader case for the abolition of copyright by appealing to a Christian notion of natural law. See Appendix C for more details.

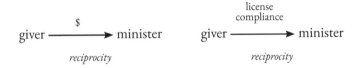

Figure 13.1: Copyright and Reciprocity

payment, can they truly say that they operate as a servant of Christ (cf. 1 Cor. 9:16)? If they impose restrictions or require payment, can they truly say that they are a servant to all so that more might be won (cf. 1 Cor. 9:19)?

To be clear, I think highly of fellow pastors who have writing ministries, many of whom engage in the kind of exchanges forbidden by the dorean principle. Most have never directly faced this issue and therefore have made their decisions in ignorance. In a sense, I hold nothing against them because I likely would have taken the same steps had I never been led to especially ruminate on the passages we've examined. However, all this being said, I cannot ignore the logical conclusion of what the Bible says about sincere ministry. From a human perspective, the error is understandable. From a divine perspective, these models of ministry culpably transgress Christ's plan for the advancement of the gospel.

While the day-to-day activities of the local church largely remain within the boundaries set by the dorean principle, the advent of the Christian publishing industry has introduced breaches of sweeping proportions. Believers who want to deepen their knowledge of the faith frequently find themselves required to give to an author or publisher (i.e., the copyright holder) before receiving the benefit of some ministry. The issue goes much further than books, encompassing

Bible study software, performance rights for worship songs, etc.

Of course, it has not always been this way. While the dorean principle has always been in danger of being violated, for the majority of the life of the church, there were relatively few opportunities for temptation or confusion to arise. However, the advancement of publication technology, especially as it has culminated in digital media, has presented the church with a test of faithfulness. Unprepared for the challenge set before her, the church has blindly followed the model of the world in its publication practices, distributing materials for a fee. Additionally, as the cost of reproduction and distribution wanes, being virtually negligible for digital content in the present era, the severity of transgression waxes stronger. Prior to the twentieth century, to purchase a book was to purchase a bound edition of printed pages. One was not paying for the content so much as they were paying for the tangible product as a whole, a matter of limited ethical concern. Today, a physical book and its content are more easily distinguished as paper and data. While people still purchase paper books, the sale of e-books indicates that publishers intend to charge not only for the physical good but also for the content. A completed work may be disseminated online to millions at no cost to the producer, yet ministering entities often default to charging for this service.

Not only does the use of copyright protection have potential to violate the dorean principle, but in most instances, it constitutes the most direct violation conceivable. Regardless of the intent of those behind such ministries, to require payment in exchange for religious education is to engage in the practices condemned by both Scripture and the early church.

Alternative Licensing

Simply stated, the antithesis of using the power of governing authorities to enforce copyright is *not* using the power of governing authorities to enforce copyright. However, under United States law, a creative work is protected by copyright as soon as it is fixed in a tangible medium. A minister who has no intention of taking advantage of

these protections must go out of his way to explicitly waive his rights
if he wishes to assure others they are free to use the creative products
of his ministry however they wish.

To that end, institutions have fashioned a variety of licenses. The
earliest of these licenses were largely designed to accommodate collab-
orative software projects,[5] but more recently, initiatives have addressed
the needs of non-software (i.e., non-functional) projects. The most
popular of these, Creative Commons, is not a single license but a
suite of licenses designed to give copyright holders the ability to mix
and match specific rights they would like to reserve or waive. Each
Creative Commons license ensures that a work may be distributed in
its original form, but additional restrictions may apply. As an exer-
cise, I'd like us to take a look at these restrictions and evaluate their
implications for dorean ministry.

Adaptation: The first option available for a Creative Commons
license is the *No Derivatives* feature. One who applies this to their
creative work restricts others from making adaptations of that work.
For a book, this would prohibit translations and audio adaptations.
For a song, this would prohibit musical rearrangements and public
performances. Anyone wishing to make such adaptations would be
required to obtain express permission from the copyright holder.

Such restrictions do not accord with the dorean principle. The
recipient of ministry should not be bound to comply with the wishes
of the minister. It is not sufficient to talk merely in terms of financial
burden; all forms of burden (i.e., direct, horizontal obligation to the
minister) fall in the same category. These stipulations do far more to
hinder the gospel than advance it.

One may object that allowing adaptations opens a work to distor-
tion and perversion. True; but at a fundamental level, *all* good things
may be corrupted. Further, the history of Christian resources testifies
that works available for adaptation encourage more good than they

---

[5]For example, the Berkeley Software Distribution (BSD) license and the GNU
General Public License (GPL) were formative for many of the similar-spirited licenses
that would follow. Major software projects have flourished under the terms of these
licenses. Recent examples of products that are partly covered by these licenses include
Android and Google Chrome.

do harm. For example, Joseph Smith (the founder of Mormonism) produced a modified version of the King James Bible in order to promote his aberrant beliefs, yet few would argue that the harm caused by this document outweighs the proliferation of the Bible in audiobooks, tracts, study Bibles, and dramatic readings, all made possible through the availability of the King James Version. Most importantly, such pragmatic objections cannot dominate the principled concern of dorean ministry.

Commercial use: Creative Commons additionally provides a *Noncommercial* feature, which prohibits use of the creative work for commercial purposes. For example, this would keep one from directly selling the licensed material, or incorporating it into a derivative work that is then sold.

From a secular perspective, this feature has received substantial pushback due to the inherent ambiguity in the concept of "commercial purposes."[6] The text of the licenses using this feature speaks specifically of uses that are "primarily intended for or directed toward commercial advantage or private monetary compensation."[7] Even if it is not sold in a traditional fashion, an entity that uses a work licensed for noncommercial use in a way that supports a commercial endeavor potentially violates the terms of the license.

Regardless, the guidelines we have already set give us a clear path forward. Restricting uses of a product of ministry, even commercial uses, does not accord with the dorean principle.

Attribution: The most commonly used option of a Creative Commons license is the *Attribution* feature. This requires that anyone distributing the original licensed work or a derivative credit the copyright holder. For example, a Bible translation licensed with this feature would require that any tract quoting it credit the copyright holder of the translation.

In several ways, this seems more reasonable than the previous restrictions we have covered. Unlike those, the requirement of attribu-

---

[6]This pushback led Creative Commons to publish a study of the public's understanding of "noncommercial use." See Creative Commons, *Defining "Noncommercial."*

[7]Creative Commons, *Attribution-NonCommercial 3.0.*

tion does not imply friction between the consumer and the copyright holder for typical adaptive uses. For the other restrictions, typical uses require explicit authorization from the copyright holder in order to proceed. Attribution, on the other hand, may be provided by anyone downstream apart from any interaction with the copyright holder.

However, from the perspective of dorean ministry, there is no reason to classify this condition as fundamentally different. Even if no money changes hands, it imposes a direct obligation on the recipient of ministry to the minister. It should therefore be rejected in the context of gospel ministry.

Naturally, the primary concerns over waiving the right to attribution center around plagiarism and misattribution. Unfortunately, the complexity of the current situation makes it difficult to provide a simple response. Copyright law is designed to address matters related to the eighth commandment (thou shalt not steal), yet it has been co-opted to address matters related to the ninth commandment (thou shalt not bear false witness). Measures to inhibit plagiarism should certainly be welcome, but it is not clear that copyright enforcement was ever the right solution. Defamation laws may offer some alternative protection and perhaps the technology of the future will provide more immediate detection of such misappropriation. Regardless, in the course of ministry, a Christian's first priority should be the honor of Christ rather than security of credit.

License propagation: A frequent feature of alternative licenses requires all derivative works, provided they are disseminated, to be made available under the terms of the same license. This is known as *copyleft*[8] and guarantees that a creative work is not used and repackaged under more restrictive terms. To this end, Creative Commons provides a *Share Alike* feature.

This particular feature does not require explicit permission from the copyright holder for typical adaptive use. Furthermore, it seems to have the added benefit of encouraging others who might use ministry materials in a similar context to embrace the same licensing scheme.

Yet once again, we must acknowledge that the *Share Alike* feature

---

[8] For the origin of this pun on "copyright," see Stallman, "The GNU Manifesto."

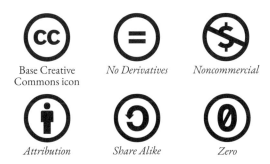

Figure 13.2: Creative Commons Icons

is a restriction that goes beyond what is permitted by the dorean principle. First, it implicitly requires the *Attribution* restriction since a license has limited significance apart from an express mention of the one issuing it. Second, it requires compliance from any producer of an adaptation.

The Public Domain

Beyond various licenses, another option exists. A *public domain* work is a work that is not subject to copyright protection. Placing a work in the public domain is not always straightforward, especially in jurisdictions that acknowledge and do not allow for the waiver of "moral rights," which include, among other things, the right to attribution. In order to provide a simple approach to this, Creative Commons offers the Creative Commons Zero Public Domain Dedication. Rather than a license, it is a waiver of rights that provides a license fallback in the event the waiver is deemed insufficient. This dedication states the intent of the author to provide maximal freedom to any consumer of the work.

In my estimation, a public domain dedication such as Creative Commons Zero offers the most consistent approach for dorean ministry. While the dorean principle does not mandate that a minister explicitly apply such a dedication to his work, it does require the spirit of such a dedication be present in all acts of gospel ministry.

Conclusion

To restrict others in their use of any product of gospel ministry is to require direct repayment—i.e., reciprocity—and violate the dorean principle. In not so many words, it says, "If I provide this ministry to you, you must do something for me." Furthermore, employing the power of governing authorities to coerce others to comply with such restrictions adds an objectionable level of hostility to the transgression.

In response, ministers and ministries should consider waiving any government-established copyright protections. For most creative works and in most jurisdictions, this may be done effectively through the use of Creative Commons Zero.

In the next chapter, I'd like us to consider some practical examples of how modern ministries use copyright, and ways to bring these practices in line with the dorean principle.

14

The Path of Progress

Problem vs. Solution

A friend of mine named Brian runs a website that displays images of ancient New Testament manuscripts. One day, he received an email from a museum demanding he pay $100 or take down his image of $\mathfrak{P}^{66}$, a fragment of John generally regarded as the oldest surviving New Testament manuscript. The museum possessed this particular relic, and in sending the message to Brian, claimed that they owned the copyright to the photographic copy featured on his site.

It's not merely hobbyist activities that are stymied by such approaches to copyright. For example, it has even had an impact on the Center for the Study of New Testament Manuscripts (CSNTM), the foremost institution in the digitization and archival of New Testament manuscripts. At a presentation from its executive director, Daniel B. Wallace, I once asked why so many of the organization's archived digitizations were inaccessible through the CSNTM website. Dr. Wallace responded by appealing to copyright and contractual agreements with the institutions that own the physical manuscripts.

The notion that copyright protects mechanical reproductions of public domain works is dubious at best, and substantial court precedent indicates otherwise.[1] Regardless, in either of these examples,

---

[1] See Dobson, "The Originality of Photographs for Purposes of Copyright

we see that the spirit of Finnian continues today. The sixth-century dispute over a copied psalter has resurfaced in our own digital era.

But as discussed in the preceding chapter, the issue goes far beyond manuscripts of Scripture. All ministry must conform to the dorean principle. In this final chapter, I'd like to begin with the production of Bible versions and continue on to address a few other areas where I believe the biblical ethic of ministry fundraising has been compromised. At each stop, I'd also like to offer some steps the church may take to restore that ethic.

Bibles

A surprising number of restrictions limit the distribution and use of Scripture. To begin, the ancient handwritten manuscripts that preserve our Old and New Testaments are largely inaccessible to the public. Many of these manuscripts hide behind physical walls because they have not been digitized, but others hide behind paywalls designed to direct revenue toward museums and other institutions.

Because manuscripts each have their own scribal peculiarities, prior to translation, Bible societies typically rescind these collected writings into a single document known as a critical edition. While legal ambiguity clouds the matter, courts outside the United States have upheld copyright protection for critical editions.[2]

Likewise, copyright protections apply to translations of Scripture. Fair use doctrine dictates that creative works may reproduce portions of other creative works for certain purposes and to limited degrees, but, at least in the United States, no law concretely codifies these limits. Due to this ambiguity, Bible version copyright holders typically provide their own guidelines, offering consumers some guarantee on what usage they will not litigate. Almost all English versions of the Bible offer roughly the same guidelines for works that incorporate them.

Law Before and After *Bridgeman Art Library, Ltd. v. Corel Corp.*"; Cameron, "In Defiance of Bridgeman."

[2] See Margoni and Perry, "Critical Editions"; Gossett, "Critical Editions."

1. The work must not be sold or used commercially. Note that the notion of commercial use typically includes practices such as featuring verses on a website that displays ads to gain revenue.

2. No more than 500 verses may be reproduced.

3. No book of the Bible may be reproduced in its entirety.

4. The reproduced text may not compose more than 25% of the work that contains it.

5. The reproduced text may not be modified from the original text of the version.

6. The version must be cited.

    a) Non-salable media such as church bulletins may simply use the appropriate version acronym (e.g., "NIV").

    b) Salable media must include a full copyright notice (typically this is roughly 25 words long). Note that items such as bookmarks, t-shirts, etc., are considered salable, even if they are not sold.

As just one example, the King James Version of the Bible (KJV) is governed by most of these standard guidelines.[3] Contrary to popular belief, the KJV does not exist in the public domain but is actually protected by the Crown's perpetual copyright, although none have attempted to enforce these restrictions outside of the United Kingdom.[4] Of course, public domain translations do exist, but these represent only a small minority of those in circulation.

Any restriction on the distribution and use of the Bible potentially harms the church. It is not merely that ministries may be inhibited from printing and distributing Bibles, but that all sorts of uses of the Bible are unduly encumbered. To publish a tract with heavy Bible usage typically requires special authorization. To fashion multi-version Bible reading software comparable to the popular options that currently exist, developers must secure rights from dozens of

---

[3]See Cambridge University Press, *Rights and Permissions*.

[4]For the history of this exclusive right, see Metzger and Coogan, *The Oxford Companion to the Bible*, 617–619.

institutions. Other potential applications share a similar overhead. Moreover, for those confused or discouraged by the proliferation of Bible versions, it is worth noting this undoubtedly exists in part *because* of restrictions imposed by copyright. Rather than pay out to other publishing houses, each publishing house with sufficient resources fashions its own version that it may use royalty-free.

Beyond these pragmatic concerns, we must ask whether a biblical principle has been violated. If the local church must minister without reciprocity, then it must have the capacity to offer the Bible without restriction. If Jesus demanded the gospel be proclaimed freely, then the gospel as recorded by his apostles should be offered without cost. Granted, the various institutions that collect manuscripts, create critical editions, and produce translations may operate only as academic enterprises, having no interest in sincere ministry. However, many of these institutions publicly state their intent to further the gospel, and inasmuch as they aim to advance the kingdom of God, they violate the dorean principle when they employ copyright protections to restrict the use of the Bible.

Books

While Bibles remain fundamental to Christian religious instruction, other books are perhaps more germane to our investigation. That is, as we have noted, one may archive biblical manuscripts, engage in textual criticism, and translate the Bible without any interest in the edification of the church. However, apart from purely academic studies, other biblical resources are almost always created with the express intent of edifying the church or reaching the lost. As such, the dorean principle especially regulates them.

Exact details on Christian publishing are difficult to come by, but in 2015, Nielson reported that adult nonfiction Christian book sales had topped 30 million units sold in 2014, rising steadily from 18 million units in 2009.[5] Even with a conservative estimate, that represents hundreds of millions of dollars a year in sales. With such

---

[5]Nielsen, *Focusing on our Strengths.*

large numbers, we should be concerned about the ethical implications for this industry.

If one sells a religious book at a price above the cost of printing, he exchanges teaching for a fee. Rather than follow the commercial publishing model of the world, ministers—i.e., Christian authors penning religious instruction—ought to give without pay because they have received without pay (cf. Matt. 10:8). Moreover, they ought not place any restriction on those who receive their teaching.

While most popular publishers require contractual agreements that would prohibit offering books freely, the present era has witnessed the rise of self-publishing. Self-publishing comes with its own drawbacks and challenges, but churches should make use of such tools if they are necessary to conform to a biblical ethic of ministry fundraising.

Similarly, academic theological publications frequently require copyright reassignment so that institutions may control access to research and to maintain streams of revenue. While the presence of open access publications has grown in some academic communities, these offerings lag behind in theological disciplines. Established journals have cultivated communities and academic integrity, but certainly, new institutions could do the same. In the meantime, Christians who want to pursue this ethic will have to pursue publishing in less highly-regarded journals or through alternative channels.

It bears repeating the insufficiency of offering such literature without financial cost. Non-financial restrictions also transgress the dorean principle. For example, a book that is offered without a fee but not licensed for modification leaves distributors unable to adapt the book to their needs. Different digital outlets might have different ways of packaging, encoding, or tagging documents, and these may be encumbered by copyright law apart from an explicit waiver. Authors seeking to minister freely should not inhibit any creative uses of their work.

The most substantial barrier to improvement in this area is that of establishment. The Christian publishing industry offers a standard, time-tested method for distributing works and recovering incurred costs. Moreover, as nearly all respectable authors of the last century have followed suit, this method has the tacit imprimatur of a host of saints. However, any who wish to sincerely honor God must not confuse a generational homogeneity with reasoned judgment. The sacred work of ministry must be distinguished from any sacred cow of method.

Music

Hymns and worship songs, while sung to the Lord, are also written for the instructional benefit of men. As such, the dorean principle must govern them. At the moment, interested parties heavily regulate Christian worship music. Many hymn lyrics are in the public domain, but typical publications of these hymns offer updated renditions subject to copyright protection. The same phenomenon occurs when published arrangements pair ancient lyrics with modern tunes. Performance of a musical work of a religious nature in the course of a service in a religious assembly does not constitute copyright infringement in the United States,[6] but most jurisdictions forbid reproduction or other public performance of these hymns without express permission. Frequently, the purchase of a hymnal grants a limited license for these activities. For churches whose singing repertoire exceeds traditional hymnody, Christian Copyright Licensing International (CCLI) manages the rights to the largest brunt of Christian worship music and issues licenses to churches and other entities.

However, even using these avenues to secure the necessary rights for congregational worship, one might be surprised at how many restrictions remain. For example, many hymnals disallow print reproduction of any kind. Additionally, licenses rarely give broad rights to record music. Furthermore, they typically prohibit changes to the musical arrangement. For example, the CCLI does not give rights to "Alter or change the lyrics, melody or fundamental character of any Song."[7] While many violate these terms in ignorance and suffer no consequences, copyright holders *have* prosecuted such cases against churches in court, even to the tune of millions of dollars in damages,

---

[6]United States Copyright Office, *Copyright Law of the United States*, 110.3.
[7]CCLI, *CCLI Copyright License Manual*.

and even for activities as seemingly innocuous as arranging a hymn for a choir.[8]

While churches could simply restrict their musical worship to songs and tunes that exist in the public domain, many regard familiarity as essential to congregational singing and would not consider such limitations a viable option. Additionally, at least in the United States, churches could rely on those provisions for religious assemblies which exempt them from the typical restrictions of the law. However, in order to remain legally compliant, they would have to be circumspect regarding the music they copy and the contexts in which they sing protected worship songs.

For the song author, the apparent solution follows those previously given. A public domain dedication removes any concerns about copyright protection, and in general, the copyright holder should not seek to take advantage of his legal position. To use the power of the civil government to enforce copyright protection on religious music is to fundamentally impose a worship tax on churches.

Software

Insofar as software marries itself to gospel ministry, the dorean principle must govern it as well. In some cases, this is more easily discerned than others.

Bible study software, since it exists solely for the purpose of religious education, ought to conform to our stated ethic. Of course, there are many applications that do not. For example, the Bible study software Logos does not include all features with anything lower than the *Gold* package, which currently retails for $1,549.99.[9] On one hand, the landscape has changed so that it has become standard for the base versions of software packages to be offered at no cost. On the other hand, these software producers often make money by upselling digital packages of licensed material specially tailored for their applications. Even public domain works retail at substantial prices. As just one

---

[8] Syn, "Copyright God," 20–21.
[9] Logos, *Logos 9 Base Packages*.

example, Logos has set the list price for their edition of John Calvin's
Institutes of the Christian Religion at $69.99.[10]

Other tools do not specifically exist for the sake of religious instruction but still attempt to provide assistance in the Christian life.
Mobile app prayer companions help Christians keep track of prayer requests, accountability software helps Christians resist temptation on
the internet, and church management systems help churches to keep
track of their resources. While the development of such applications
may not be an activity that proclaims the gospel or directly attends to
its proclamation, Christians should think twice before charging for
such tools. Recall that the disciples were forbidden from charging for
healing (Matt. 10:8), and many of these tools aim to effect a sort of
healing in the life of the user, that they might better know the grace
of Christ.

Anything governed by the dorean principle should be offered
freely, without restriction. In the context of software, this not only
implies access to an application but also the permission to modify
it. Developers designing applications in an attempt to further the
gospel should take this into account and write such adaptable software,
typically styled *open source*.

Conclusion

In the modern age, copyright presents the greatest threat to the dorean
principle. However, there is hope. We do not have to be stuck in the
age of Colmcille and his fettered psalter. In each of the categories
presented in this chapter, the church has the opportunity to move
forward by embracing support models that revolve around colabor
and abandon attempts to secure reciprocity.

---

[10] Logos, *Institutes of the Christian Religion*.

Conclusion

A Final Word About the Gospel

The prophet Isaiah describes salvation as water that is offered "without money and without price" (Isa. 55:1). In the gospels, Jesus explains he is the source of that living water (John 7:37). On the final pages of Scripture, John records the repeated assertion that the Lord offers this water freely (Rev. 21:6; 22:17). As we consider the relationship between money and ministry, there is nothing less at stake than the proper advancement of the gospel of Jesus Christ.

If the dorean principle correctly summarizes the ministry fundraising ethic of the New Testament, the implications are far-reaching. In regular church work and activity, this truth may round out some rough edges, but in other areas, it demands radical transformation. Equipped with this one maxim, we may curb the commercialization of Christianity and usher in a new era of uncompromised ministry.

> *In the context of gospel proclamation, accepting support as anything other than an act of colabor compromises the sincerity of ministry.*

The modern church has unintentionally gone astray, blindly following the model of the world. What blessings await if we will reform our practices, calling ministers and ministries to repentance?

> *Its heads give judgment for a bribe;*
> *its priests teach for a price;*
> *its prophets practice divination for money;*

yet they lean on the Lord and say,
   "Is not the Lord in the midst of us?
   No disaster shall come upon us." (Mic. 3:11)

Appendix A

Further Study

I wrote this little book to be an accessible version of a thesis I wrote for a Master of Divinity degree. If this book has fascinated you and you would like to dive deeper, I would recommend beginning with that thesis and consulting the bibliography. Every topic featured in this book appears in the thesis with extended detail and argument. Additionally, it covers some topics I have chosen not to address here.

For example, the thesis contains the following explorations:

- a deeper analysis of 1 Corinthians and Paul's concern over matters of conscience

- a dedicated treatment of each of the four apparent discrepancies in Paul's financial policy

- a presentation of the Jerusalem collection as an exemplary act of colabor

- a biblical theology of colabor

- an analysis of objections to pastoral salaries during the time of the Reformation and in the modern era

- an extended examination of the copyright issues surrounding biblical manuscripts, critical editions, and translations

The thesis may be found at thedoreanprinciple.org.

Appendix B

Copyright in the United States

In the United States,[1] copyright applies to original works fixed in a tangible medium of expression. It may additionally apply to various artistic works but does not protect facts or inventions. Works exist under copyright protection the moment they are fixed in a tangible form. One may register a work with the U.S. Copyright Office, but this registration is unnecessary to establish protection, only to assist in the event of litigation.

Copyright protection provides the copyright holder with exclusive rights to reproduce the original work, make derivative works, distribute copies of a work, or display or perform that work publicly. However, fair use doctrine allows for segments of a protected work to be copied and distributed for purposes such as criticism. Copyright protection lasts for the life of the author plus an additional 70 years. For anonymous works or works made for hire, it typically endures for 95 years from initial publication.

The Digital Millennium Copyright Act (DMCA) enacted in 1998 provides additional protections or limitations on digital works. Because digital works often include some copy protection mecha-

---

[1] The following information is summarized from United States Copyright Office, *Copyright Law of the United States.*

nism, the DMCA makes it illegal to circumvent these mechanisms or to disseminate tools intended to circumvent these mechanisms. Additionally, the DMCA makes it illegal to link to infringing content. Because many service providers (e.g., online video sites) host content uploaded by users, the DMCA offers a provision to grant safe harbor for such utilities, provided they comply with regulations designed to prevent copyright infringement.

Of course, there are many details and edge cases not covered in this brief summary. Furthermore, copyright law in the United States has a varied history, so these rules do not apply uniformly to works authored in the past.

Appendix C

Copyright and Natural Law

In Chapter 13, I argued that the dorean principle should lead ministers to forgo legal enforcement of copyright protections in the context of ministry. However, there is a stronger case to be made that all Christians should waive such protections in all contexts. While theologians differ on the matter, I would argue that a biblical view of natural law delegitimizes the entire notion of intellectual property.

First, it should be recognized that copyright law is an artificial imposition on the economy of creative works. In the words of Christopher May and Susan K. Sell, "Intellectual property constructs a scarce resource from knowledge or information that is not formally scarce."[1] Ideas are inherently reproducible, and in a digital age, the cost of reproducing most works is negligible. However, copyright protection maintains an economy around the selling and buying of licenses to obtain copies of creative works and the rights to use them.

Beyond this initial observation, the relatively recent advent of copyright regulations demonstrates their nature as purely human inventions.[2] If they were instead codifications of a divine principle, one would expect such statutes to appear earlier in human history. Additionally, while most relevant laws protect material property to

---

[1] C. May and Sell, *Intellectual Property Rights*, 5.

[2] The Statute of Anne (1710) was the first legislated copyright protection to be enforced by public courts.

perpetuity, the copyright protection offered by governments is—in all but a few circumstances—temporary. This constitutes an implicit concession that "intellectual property" is not property in the truest sense. The fact that some of these protections last for twenty years and some longer than a lifetime testify to the arbitrary nature of intellectual property law.

Of course, not all would agree. Some have argued that copyright protection stems from *natural rights*, those rights given by God. In fact, the founding fathers of the United States incorporated provisions for intellectual property law in the constitution on the basis of a Lockean understanding of natural rights.[3] If one has a right to liberty and property, the body being irrevocably the property of the individual, then he has a right to the products of his body, the fruit of his labors. Moreover, one who goes about the improvement of nature ought to be able to reap the rewards of that improvement. Following this line of reasoning, one may conclude that no categorical difference exists between intellectual property and material property; one who fashions a creative work ought to have ownership over it as his own property.

While these Lockean premises are unobjectionable, the conclusion must be questioned. To protect the product of the mind, is not the right to hold a secret sufficient? One who is not compelled to divulge information or share property may keep his creative works to himself. However, once disseminated, he has freely given this information to the public. With material property, a violation of the eighth commandment (thou shalt not steal) results in direct loss for another individual. With intellectual property, undesired copying and use of a published work may only be counted as a loss when estimating the potential of an idea to garner profit. In the words of Thomas Jefferson:

> If nature has made any one thing less susceptible than all others of exclusive property, it is the action of the thinking power called an idea, which an individual may exclu-

---

[3]See R. J. May and Cooper, *The Constitutional Foundations of Intellectual Property*.

sively possess as long as he keeps it to himself; but the moment it is divulged, it forces itself into the possession of every one, and the receiver cannot dispossess himself of it. Its peculiar character, too, is that no one possesses the less, because every other possesses the whole of it. He who receives an idea from me, receives instruction himself without lessening mine; as he who lights his taper at mine, receives light without darkening me. That ideas should freely spread from one to another over the globe, for the moral and mutual instruction of man, and improvement of his condition, seems to have been peculiarly and benevolently designed by nature, when she made them, like fire, expansible over all space, without lessening their density in any point, and like the air in which we breathe, move and have our physical being, incapable of confinement or exclusive appropriation.[4]

In my estimation, the language employed in copyright legislation betrays the underlying utilitarian motives. The U.S. Constitution gives Congress the power "To promote the Progress of Science and useful Arts, by securing for limited Times to Authors and Inventors the exclusive Right to their respective Writings and Discoveries." The Statute of Anne established copyright law "for preventing [the detriment of authors and proprietors] for the future, and for the encouragement of learned men to compose and write useful books." Rather than flowing from natural rights endowed by our Creator, copyright law arises from a pragmatic desire to model the economy of creative works after the economy of physical goods.

If it can be granted that the government has a sweeping authority to wield its power to improve the lives of its subjects, modern copyright may have some place in society. If instead the God-ordained authority of the civil magistrate is limited to the enforcement of retributive justice, the government may only prosecute those who have violated the natural rights of another. In this view, *lex talionis* (Ex. 21:24) combined with the Deuteronomic principle that justice shall

---

[4]Jefferson, *Letter to Isaac McPherson (1813)*.

not be perverted by other prerogatives (Deut. 16:17–20) restricts governing authorities from erecting legislation extraneous to the violation of one's property rights.

If copyright is not a natural right, then its protection is not a legitimate function of government. If copyright is not a natural right, then it is unethical for any man or ministry to use the power of the government in a court of law to enforce copyright. In fact, rather than a protection of the copyright holders' rights, such an action would be a violation of the consumers' rights, as they ought to be able to do as they please with the information in their possession.[5]

---

[5] For fuller arguments from similar perspectives, see Kinsella, *Against Intellectual Property*; Poythress, *Copyright and Copying*.

Bibliography

Athanasius. *Letter 39*.

Bauckham, Richard J. *Jude, 2 Peter*. Vol. 50. WBC. Word Books, 1983.

Bauer, Walter. *A Greek-English Lexicon of the New Testament and Other Early Christian Literature, Third Edition*. Ed. by Frederick William Danker. The University of Chicago Press, 2000.

Blomberg, Craig L. *Matthew*. Vol. 22. The New American Commentary. B&H Academic, 1992.

— *Neither Poverty nor Riches. A Biblical Theology of Possessions*. Ed. by D. A. Carson. NSBT. InterVarsity Press, 1999.

Bock, Darrell L. *Acts*. BECNT. Baker Academic, 2007.

Briones, David E. *Paul's Financial Policy. A Socio-Theological Approach*. Library of New Testament Studies. Bloomsbury T&T Clark, 2013.

— "Paul's Intentional 'Thankless Thanks' in Philippians 4.10–20." In: *Journal for the Study of the New Testament* 34 (1 2011), pp. 47–69.

Bruce, F.F. *The Book of the Acts*. NICNT. William B. Eerdmans Publishing Company, 1988.

Cambridge University Press. *Rights and Permissions*. URL: https://www.cambridge.org/bibles/about/rights-and-permissions/ (visited on 03/09/2019).

Cameron, Colin T. "In Defiance of Bridgeman. Claiming Copyright in Photographic Reproductions of Public Domain Works." In: *Texas Intellectual Property Law Journal* 15 (1 Sept. 2006), pp. 31–61.

Carson, D. A. *When Jesus Confronts the World*. Authentic Media, 1987.

CCLI. *CCLI Copyright License Manual*. URL: https://us.ccli.com/manual/ (visited on 03/20/2019).

Corrigan, Ray. "Colmcille and the Battle of the Book. Technology, Law and Access to Knowledge in 6th Century Ireland." In: *GikII 2 Workshop on the intersections between law, technology and popular culture at University College London* (Sept. 2007).

Creative Commons. *Attribution-NonCommercial 3.0*. URL:
    https://creativecommons.org/licenses/by-nc/3.0/us/legalcode
    (visited on 02/04/2019).

— *Defining "Noncommercial." A Study of How the Online Population
    Understands "Noncommercial Use."* Creative Commons Corporation,
    2009.

Cru. *2018 Annual Report*. URL:
    https://www.cru.org/content/dam/cru/about/2018-cru-annual-
    report.pdf (visited on 05/30/2020).

Dobson, Kimberly N. "The Originality of Photographs for Purposes of
    Copyright Law Before and After *Bridgeman Art Library, Ltd. v. Corel
    Corp.*" In: *Florida Coastal Law Review* 10 (2 Winter 2009), pp. 319–347.

Downs, David J. *The Offering of the Gentiles. Paul's Collection for Jerusalem
    in Its Chronological, Cultural, and Cultic Contexts*. Mohr Siebeck, 2008.

Eusebius. "Church History." In: *Nicene and Post-Nicene Fathers, Series II*.
    Vol. 1. Christian Literature Publishing Co., 1890, pp. 3–402.

Fee, Gordon D. "ΧΑΡΙΣ in II Corinthians I.15. Apostolic Parousia and
    Paul-Corinth Chronology." In: *New Testament Studies* 24 (4 July 1978),
    pp. 533–538.

— *The First Epistle to the Corinthians*. NICNT. William B. Eerdmans
    Publishing Company, 2013.

Garland, David E. *1 Corinthians*. BECNT. Baker Academic, 2003.

Ginzberg, Louis. *The Legends of the Jews*. The Jewish Publication Society of
    America, 1913.

Gonzalez, Justo L. *Faith and Wealth. A History of Early Christian Ideas on
    the Origin, Use, and Significance of Money*. Wipf & Stock Publishers,
    1990.

González, Justo L. "New Testament Koinónia and Wealth." In: *Missions
    and Money*. Ed. by Jonathan J. Bonk. Vol. 15. American Society of
    Missiology Series. Orbis Books, 2006, pp. 203–221.

Gospel in Life. *Tim Keller MP3 Sermon Archive*. July 22, 2020. URL: https:
    //gospelinlife.com/downloads/timothy-keller-mp3-sermon-archive/
    (visited on 01/27/2020).

Gossett, Philip. "Critical Editions. Musicologists and Copyright." In: *Fontes
    Artis Musicae* 52 (3 July 2005), pp. 139–144.

Hansen, Collin. "Piper on Pastors' Pay." In: (Nov. 6, 2013). URL:
    https://www.thegospelcoalition.org/article/piper-on-pastors-pay/
    (visited on 02/18/2019).

Harris, Murray J. *The Second Epistle to the Corinthians*. NIGTC. William B.
    Eerdmans Publishing Company, 2005.

Harvey, A. E. "The Workman is Worthy of His Hire. Fortunes of a Proverb in the Early Church." In: *Novum Testamentum* 24 (3 1982), pp. 209–221.

Hock, R. F. "The Working Apostle. An Examination of Paul's Means of Livelihood." PhD thesis. Yale University, 1974.

Hooker, Morna D. "A Partner in the Gospel. Paul's Understanding of His Ministry." In: *Theology and Ethics in Paul and His Interpreters.* Abingdon Press, 1996, pp. 83–100.

Jamieson, Robert, A. R. Fausset, and David Brown. *A Commentary, Critical, Practical, and Explanatory, on the Old and New Testaments.* Fleming H. Revell, 1880.

Jefferson, Thomas. *Letter to Isaac McPherson (1813).*

Jefford, Clayton N. "Did Ignatius of Antioch Know the Didache?" In: *The Didache in Context. Essays on Its Text, History and Transmission.* Ed. by Clayton N. Jefford. E.J. Brill, 1995, pp. 330–351.

Keller, Timothy. *Every Good Endeavor. Connecting Your Work to God's Work.* Penguin, 2014.

Kinsella, N. Stephan. *Against Intellectual Property.* Ludwig von Mises Institute, 2008.

Kumar, Anugrah. "Joel Osteen's Lakewood Church Has Annual Budget of $90 Million: Here's How That Money Is Spent." In: *The Christian Post* (June 3, 2014).

Laura, Robert. *Pastor Rick Warren Is Well Prepared For A Purpose Driven Retirement.* Mar. 21, 2013. URL: https: //www.forbes.com/sites/robertlaura/2013/03/21/pastor-rick-warren-is-practicing-what-he-preaches-and-getting-ready-for-retirement/ (visited on 02/18/2019).

Lightfoot, J. B. *The Apostolic Fathers.* Macmillan and Co., Limited, 1912.

Logos. *Institutes of the Christian Religion.* URL: https: //www.logos.com/product/16036/institutes-of-the-christian-religion (visited on 06/18/2021).

— *Logos 9 Base Packages.* URL: https://www.logos.com/basepackages (visited on 06/18/2021).

Luther, Martin. *A Commentary on St. Paul's Epistle to the Galatians.* Zondervan, 1939.

— *Commentary on Peter and Jude.* Kregel Classics, 2005.

— *First Principles of the Reformation.* William Clowes and Sons, Limited, 1883.

Margoni, Thomas and Mark Perry. "Critical Editions. An Example of European Copyright Law (Dis)Harmonization." In: *Canadian Intellectual Property Review* 27 (Nov. 2011), pp. 157–170.

May, Christopher and Susan K. Sell. *Intellectual Property Rights. A Critical History*. Lynne Rienner Publishers, 2006.

May, Randolph J. and Seth L. Cooper. *The Constitutional Foundations of Intellectual Property. A Natural Rights Perspective*. Carolina Academic Press, 2015.

Metzger, Bruce M. and Michael David Coogan. *The Oxford Companion to the Bible*. Oxford University Press, 1993.

Milavec, Aaron. *The Didache. Text, Translation, Analysis, and Commentary*. Liturgical Press, 2003.

Moo, Douglas J. *The Epistle to the Romans*. NICNT. William B. Eerdmans Publishing Company, 1996.

— *The Letters to the Colossians and to Philemon*. PNTC. William B. Eerdmans Publishing Company, 2008.

Niederwimmer, Kurt. *The Didache*. Hermeneia. Fortress Press, 1998.

Nielsen. *Focusing on our Strengths. Key Insights into the Christian Market from Nielsen Book*. URL: https://www.nielsen.com/us/en/insights/reports/2015/focusing-on-our-strengths-insights-into-the-christian-book-market.html (visited on 05/30/2020).

Nolland, John. *The Gospel of Matthew*. NIGTC. William B. Eerdmans Publishing Company, 2005.

Ogereau, Julien M. *Paul's Koinonia with the Philippians. A Socio-Historical Investigation of a Pauline Economic Partnership*. WUNT. Mohr Siebeck, 2014.

Origen. "Against Celsus." In: *Ante-Nicene Fathers*. Ed. by Philip Schaff. Vol. 4. William B. Eerdmans Publishing Company, 1885, pp. 395–669.

Orr, William F. and James Arthur Walther. *I Corinthians*. The Anchor Yale Bible Commentaries. Doubleday & Company, Inc, 1976.

Osiek, Carolyn. *The Shepherd of Hermas*. Hermeneia. Fortress Press, 1999.

Owens, Conley. "Divine Mediation in Paul's Financial Policy." In: *Theolog* (Jan. 2021), pp. 67–78.

Patterson, Stephen J. "The Legacy of Radical Itinerancy in Early Christianity." In: *The Didache in Context. Essays on Its Text, History and Transmission*. Ed. by Clayton N. Jefford. E.J. Brill, 1995, pp. 313–329.

Peterman, Gerald W. "'Thankless Thanks': The Epistolary Social
    Convention In Philippians 4:10–20." In: *Tyndale Bulletin* 42 (2 1991),
    pp. 261–270.

Plass, Ewald. *What Luther Says*. Concordia Publishing House, 1959.

Poythress, Vern. *Copyright and Copying. Why The Laws Should Be
    Changed*. URL: https://frame-poythress.org/copyrights-and-copying-
    why-the-laws-should-be-changed/ (visited on 05/23/2020).

Richards, E. Randolph. *Paul and First-Century Letter Writing. Secretaries,
    Composition and Collection*. InterVarsity Press, 2004.

Roberts, Alexander and James Donaldson. *The Ante-Nicene Fathers*. Vol. 7.
    The Christian Literature Company, 1886.

RTS. *Master of Divinity*. URL: https://rts.edu/degree/mdiv/ (visited on
    06/17/2021).

— *Tuition and Fees*. URL: https://rts.edu/admissions/tuition/ (visited on
    06/17/2021).

Sampley, J. Paul. *Pauline Partnership in Christ*. Fortress Press, 1980.

Schütz, John Howard. *Paul and the Anatomy of Apostolic Authority*. The
    New Testament Library. Westminster John Knox Press, 2007.

Stallman, Richard M. "The GNU Manifesto." In: *Dr. Dobb's Journal of
    Software Tools* 10.3 (Mar. 1995), pp. 30–35.

Syn, Roger. "Copyright God. Enforcement of Copyright in the Bible and
    Religious Works." In: *Regent University Law Review* 14 (1 2001–2003),
    pp. 1–34.

Tertullian. "Apology." In: *Ante-Nicene Fathers*. Ed. by Philip Schaff. Vol. 3.
    William B. Eerdmans Publishing Company, 1885, pp. 17–60.

The Summit Church. *Easter at the Summit*. URL:
    https://summitchurch.com/easter (visited on 04/20/2019).

Theissen, Gerd. *Fortress Introduction to the New Testament*. Fortress Press,
    2003.

— "Legitimation and Subsistence. An Essay on the Sociology of Early
    Christian Missionaries." In: *The Social Setting of Pauline Christianity.
    Essays on Corinth*. Fortress Press, 1982, pp. 27–68.

— "Social Stratification in the Corinthian Community. A Contribution
    to the Sociology of Early Hellenistic Christianity." In: *The Social
    Setting of Pauline Christianity. Essays on Corinth*. Fortress Press, 1982,
    pp. 69–120.

Together for the Gospel. *Together for the Gospel*. URL: https://t4g.org/
    (visited on 04/15/2020).

United States Copyright Office. *Copyright Law of the United States. and Related Laws Contained in Title 17 of the United States Code*. United States Copyright Office, 2016.

Varner, William. "The Didache's Use of the Old and New Testaments." In: *TMSJ* 16.1 (May 2005), pp. 127–151.

Verbrugge, Verlyn D. and Keith R. Krell. *Paul and Money. A Biblical and Theological Analysis of the Apostle's Teachings and Practices*. Zondervan, 2015.

Waldron, Samuel E. "A Careful Exposition of 1 Timothy 5:17." In: *In Defense of Parity. A Presentation of the Parity or Equality of Elders in the New Testament*. Truth for Eternity Ministries, 1997, pp. 75–95.

Subject Index

Scripture Index